Life of
Robert Burns

MOSTLY BY
Thomas Carlyle.

EDITOR'S PREFACE.

The readers of the "Household Library" will certainly welcome a Life of Burns. That his soul was of the real heroic stamp, no one who is familiar with his imperishable lyric poetry, will deny.

This Life of the great Scottish bard is composed of two parts. The first part, which is brief, and gives merely his external life, is taken from the "Encyclopedia Britannica." The principle object of it, in this place, is to prepare the reader for what follows. The second part is a grand spiritual portrait of Burns, the like of which the ages have scarcely produced; the equal of which, in our opinion, does not exist. In fact, since men began to write and publish their thoughts in this world, no one has appeared who equals Carlyle as a spiritual-portrait painter; and, taken all in all, this of his gifted countryman Burns is his master-piece. I should not dare to say how many times I have perused it, and always with new wonder and delight. I once read it in the Manfrini Palace, at Venice, sitting before Titian's portrait of Ariosto. Great is the contrast between the Songs of Burns and the *Rime* of the Italian poet, between the fine spiritual perception of Carlyle's mind and the delicate touch of Titian's hand, between picturesque expression and an expressive picture; yet this very antithesis seemed to prepare my mind for the full enjoyment of both these famous portraits; the sombre majesty of northern genius seemed to heighten and be heightened by the sunset glow of the genius of the south.

Besides giving the article from the "Encyclopedia Britannica," as a kind of frame for the portrait of Burns, we will here add, from the "English Cyclopedia," a sketch of Carlyle's life. A severe taste may find it a little out of place, yet we must be allowed to consult the wishes of those for whom these little volumes are designed.

Carlyle, (Thomas,) a thinker and writer, confessedly among the most original and influential that Britain has produced, was born in the parish of Middlebie, near the village of Ecclefechan, in Dumfries-shire, Scotland, on the 4th of December, 1795. His father, a man of remarkable force of character, was a small farmer in comfortable circumstances; his mother was also no ordinary person. The eldest son of a considerable family, he received an education the best in its kind that Scotland could then afford— the education of a pious and industrious home, supplemented by that of school and college. (Another son of the family, Dr. John A. Carlyle, a younger brother of Thomas, was educated in a similar manner, and, after practising for many years as a physician in Germany and Rome, has recently become known in British literature as the author of the best prose translation of Dante.) After a few years spent at the ordinary parish school, Thomas was sent, in his thirteenth or fourteenth year, to the grammar school of the neighboring town of Annan; and here it was that he first became acquainted with a man destined, like himself, to a career of great celebrity. "The first time I saw Edward Irving," writes Mr. Carlyle in 1835, "was six-and-twenty years ago, in his native town, Annan. He was fresh from Edinburgh, with college prizes, high character, and promise: he had come to see our school-master, who had also been his. We heard of famed professors—of high matters, classical, mathematical—a whole Wonderland of knowledge; nothing but joy, health, hopefulness without end, looked out from the blooming young man." Irving was then sixteen years of age, Carlyle fourteen; and from that time till Irving's sad and premature death, the two were intimate and constant friends. It was not long before Carlyle followed Irving to that "Wonderland of Knowledge," the University of Edinburgh, of which, and its "famed professors," he had received such tidings. If the description of the nameless German university, however, in "Sartor Resartus," is to be supposed as allusive also to Mr. Carlyle's own reminiscences of his training at Edinburgh, he seems afterwards to have held the more formal or academic part of that training in no very high respect. "What vain jargon of controversial metaphysic, etymology, and mechanical

4

manipulation, falsely named science, was current there," says Teufelsdröckh; "I indeed learned better perhaps than most." At Edinburgh, the professor of "controversial metaphysic" in Carlyle's day, was Dr. Thomas Brown, Dugald Stewart having then just retired; physical science and mathematics, were represented by Playfair and Sir John Leslie, and classical studies by men less known to fame. While at college, Carlyle's special bent, so far as the work of the classes was concerned, seems to have been to mathematics and natural philosophy. But it is rather by his voluntary studies and readings, apart from the work of the classes, that Mr. Carlyle, in his youth, laid the foundation of his vast and varied knowledge. The college session in Edinburgh extends over about half the year, from November to April; and during these months, the college library, and other such libraries as were accessible, were laid under contribution by him to an extent till then hardly paralleled by any Scottish student. Works on science and mathematics, works on philosophy, histories of all ages, and the great classics of British literature, were read by him miscellaneously or in orderly succession; and it was at this period, also, if we are not mistaken, he commenced his studies—not very usual then in Scotland—in the foreign languages of modern Europe. With the same diligence, and in very much the same way, were the summer vacations employed, during which he generally returned to his father's house in Dumfries-shire, or rambled among the hills and moors of that neighborhood.

Mr. Carlyle had begun his studies with a view to entering the Scottish Church. About the time, however, when these studies were nearly ended, and when, according to the ordinary routine, he might have become a preacher, a change of views induced him to abandon the intended profession. This appears to have been about the year 1819 or 1820, when he was twenty-four years of age. For some time, he seems to have been uncertain as to his future course. Along with Irving, he employed himself for a year or two, as a teacher in Fifeshire; but gradually it became clear to him, that his true vocation was that of literature. Accordingly, parting from Irving, about the year 1822, the younger Scot of

Annandale, deliberately embraced the alternative open to him, and became a general man of letters. Probably few have ever embraced that profession with qualifications so wide, or with aims so high and severe. Apart altogether from his diligence in learning, and from the extraordinary amount of acquired knowledge of all kinds, which was the fruit of it, there had been remarked in him, from the first, a strong originality of character, a noble earnestness and fervor in all that he said or did, and a vein of inherent constitutional contempt for the mean and the frivolous, inclining him, in some degree, to a life of isolation and solitude. Add to this, that his acquaintance with German literature, in particular, had familiarized him with ideas, modes of thinking, and types of literary character, not then generally known in this country, and yet, in his opinion, more deserving of being known than much of a corresponding kind that was occupying and ruling British thought.

The first period of Mr. Carlyle's literary life may be said to extend from 1822 to 1827, or from his twenty-sixth to his thirty-second year. It was during this period that he produced (besides a translation of Legendre's "Geometry," to which he prefixed an "Essay on Proportion,") his numerous well-known translations from German writers, and also his "Life of Schiller." The latter and a considerable proportion of the former, were written by him during the leisure afforded him by an engagement he had formed in 1823, as tutor to Charles Buller, whose subsequent brilliant though brief career in the politics of Britain, gives interest to this connection. The first part of the "Life of Schiller" appeared originally in the "London Magazine," of which John Scott was editor, and Hazlitt, Charles Lamb, Allan Cunningham, De Quincey, and Hood, were the best known supporters; and the second and third parts, were published in the same magazine in 1824. In this year appeared also the translation of Göthe's "Wilhelm Meister," which was published by Messrs. Oliver and Boyd, of Edinburgh, without the translator's name. This translation, the first real introduction of Göthe to the reading world of Great Britain, attracted much notice. "The translator," said a critic in "Blackwood," "is, we understand, a young gentleman in this city, who now for the first time appears before the public. We congratulate him on his very promising debut; and would fain hope to receive a series of really good translations from his hand. He has evidently a perfect knowledge of German; he already writes English better than is at all common, even at this time; and we know of no exercise more likely to produce effects of permanent advantage upon a young mind of intellectual ambition." The advice here given to Mr. Carlyle by his critic, was followed by him in so far that, in 1827, he published in Edinburgh, his "Specimens of German Romance," in four volumes; one of these containing "Wilhelm Meister's Wanderjahre," as a fresh specimen of Göthe; the others containing tales from Jean Paul, Tieck, Musæus, and Hoffman. Meanwhile, in 1825, Mr. Carlyle had revised and enlarged his "Life of Schiller," and given it to the world in a separate form, through the press of Messrs. Taylor and Hessay, the proprietors of the "London Magazine." In the same year, quitting his tutorship of Charles Buller, he had married a lady fitted in a pre-eminent degree to be the wife of such a man. (It is interesting to know that Mrs. Carlyle, originally Miss Welch, is a lineal descendent of the Scottish Reformer, Knox.) For some time after the marriage, Mr. Carlyle continued to reside in Edinburgh; but before 1827 he removed to Craigenputtoch, a small property in the most solitary part of Dumfries-shire.

The second period of Mr. Carlyle's literary life, extending from 1827 to 1834, or from his thirty-second to his thirty-ninth year, was the period of the first decided manifestations of his extraordinary originality as a thinker. Probably the very seclusion in which he lived helped to develope, in stronger proportions, his native and peculiar tendencies. The following account of his place and mode of life at this time was sent by him, in 1828, to Göthe, with whom he was then in correspondence, and was published by the great German in the preface to a German translation of the "Life of Schiller," executed under his immediate care:—
"Dumfries is a pleasant town, containing about fifteen thousand

inhabitants, and to be considered the centre of the trade and judicial system of a district which possesses some importance in the sphere of Scottish activity. Our residence is not in the town itself, but fifteen miles to the northwest of it, among the granite hills and the black morasses which stretch westward through Galloway almost to the Irish Sea. In this wilderness of heath and rock, our estate stands forth a green oasis, a tract of ploughed, partly inclosed and planted ground, where corn ripens and trees afford a shade, although surrounded by sea-mews and rough-woolled sheep. Here, with no small effort, have we built and furnished a neat, substantial dwelling; here, in the absence of a professional or other office, we live to cultivate literature according to our strength, and in our own peculiar way. We wish a joyful growth to the roses and flowers of our garden; we hope for health and peaceful thoughts to further our aims. The roses, indeed, are still in part to be planted, but they blossom already in anticipation. Two ponies which carry us every where, and the mountain air, are the best medicine for weak nerves. This daily exercise, to which I am much devoted, is my only recreation; for this nook of ours is the loneliest in Britain—six miles removed from any one likely to visit me. Here Rousseau would have been as happy as on his island of Saint-Pierre. My town friends, indeed, ascribe my sojourn here to a similar disposition, and forbode me no good result; but I came hither solely with the design to simplify my way of life, and to secure the independence through which I could be enabled to remain true to myself. This bit of earth is our own; here we can live, write, and think, as best pleases ourselves, even though Zoilus himself were to be crowned the monarch of literature. Nor is the solitude of such great importance, for a stage-coach takes us speedily to Edinburgh, which we look upon as our British Weimar; and have I not, too, at this moment, piled upon the table of my little library, a whole cart-load of French, German, American, and English journals and periodicals—whatever may be their worth? Of antiquarian studies, too, there is no lack."

Before this letter was written, Mr. Carlyle had already begun the well-known series of his contributions to the "Edinburgh Review." The first of these was his essay on "Jean Paul," which appeared in 1827; and was followed by his striking article on "German Literature," and by his singularly beautiful essay on "Burns" (1828). Other essays in the same periodical followed, as well as articles in the "Foreign Quarterly Review," which was established in 1828, and shorter articles of less importance in Brewster's "Edinburgh Encyclopedia," then in course of publication. Externally, in short, at this time, Mr. Carlyle was a writer for reviews and magazines, choosing to live, for the convenience of his work and the satisfaction of his own tastes, in a retired nook of Scotland, whence he could correspond with his friends, occasionally visit the nearest of them, and occasionally also receive visits from them in turn. Among the friends whom he saw in his occasional visits to Edinburgh, were Jeffrey, Wilson, and other literary celebrities of that capital (Sir Walter Scott, we believe, he never met otherwise than casually in the streets); among the more distant friends who visited him, none was more welcome than the American Emerson, who, having already been attracted to him by his writings, made a journey to Dumfries-shire, during his first visit to England, expressly to see him; and of his foreign correspondents, the most valued by far was Göthe, whose death in 1832, and that of Scott in the same year, impressed him deeply, and were finely commemorated by him.

Meanwhile, though thus ostensibly but an occasional contributor to periodicals, Mr. Carlyle was silently throwing his whole strength into a work which was to reveal him in a far other character than that of a mere literary critic, however able and profound. This was his "Sartor Resartus;" or, an imaginary History of the Life and Opinions of Herr Teufelsdröckh, an eccentric German professor and philosopher. Under this quaint guise (the name "Sartor Resartus" being, it would appear, a translation into Latin of "The Tailor done over," which is the title of an old Scottish song), Mr. Carlyle propounded, in a style half-serious and half-grotesque, and in a manner far more bold and trenchant than the rules of review-writing permitted, his own philosophy of life and society in almost all their bearings. The work was truly an anomaly in British literature, exhibiting a combination of deep, speculative power, poetical genius, and lofty moral purpose, with wild and riotous humor and shrewd observation and satire, such as had rarely been seen; and coming into the midst of the more conventional British literature of the day, it was like a fresh but barbaric blast from the hills and moorlands amid which it had been conceived. But the very strangeness and originality of the work prevented it from finding a publisher; and after the manuscript had been returned by several London firms to whom it was offered, the author was glad to cut it into parts and publish it piecemeal in "Frazer's Magazine." Here it appeared in the course of 1833-34, scandalising most readers by its Gothic mode of thought and its extraordinary torture, as it was called, of the English language; but eagerly read by some sympathetic minds, who discerned in the writer a new power in literature, and wondered who and what he was.

With the publication of the "Sartor Resartus" papers, the third period of Mr. Carlyle's literary life may be said to begin. It was during the negotiations for the publication that he was led to contemplate removing to London—a step which he finally took, we believe, in 1834. Since that year—the thirty-ninth of his life—Mr. Carlyle has permanently resided in London, in a house situated in one of the quiet streets running at right angles to the River Thames, at Chelsea. The change into the bustle of London, from the solitude of Craigenputtoch was, externally, a great one. In reality, however, it was less than it seemed. A man in the prime of life, when he came to reside in the metropolis, he brought into its roar and confusion, not the restless spirit of a young adventurer, but the settled energy of one who had ascertained his strength, and fixed his methods and his aims.

Among the Maginns and others who contributed to "Frazer," he at once took his place as a man rather to influence than be influenced; and gradually, as the circle of his acquaintances widened so as to include such notable men as John

Mill, Sterling, Maurice, Leigh Hunt, Browning, Thackeray, and others of established or rising fame in all walks of speculation and literature, the recognition of his rare personal powers of influence became more general and deep. In particular, in that London circle, in which John Sterling moved, was his personal influence great, even while as yet he was but the anonymous author of the "Sartor Resartus" papers, and of numerous other contributions, also anonymous, to "Frazer's Magazine," and the "Edinburgh," "Foreign Quarterly," "British and Foreign," and "Westminster," Reviews. It was not till 1837, or his forty-second year, that his name, already so well known to an inner circle of admirers, was openly associated with a work fully proportional to his powers. This was his "French Revolution: a History," in three volumes, the extraordinary merits of which as at once a history and a gorgeous prose-epic, are known to all. In 1838, the "Sartor Resartus" papers, already re-published in the United States, were put forth, collectively, with his name; and, in the same year, his various scattered articles in periodicals, after having similarly received the honor of re-publication in America, were given to the world in four volumes, in their chronological series from 1827 to 1837, under the title of "Miscellanies." Mr. Carlyle's next publication was his little tract on "Chartism," published in 1839, in which, to use the words of one of his critics, "he first broke ground on the Condition of England question."

During the time when these successive publications were carrying his name through the land, Mr. Carlyle appeared in a new capacity, and delivered four courses of lectures in London to select but crowded audiences, including many of the aristocracy both of rank and of literature: the first, a course on "German Literature," delivered at Willis's Rooms in 1837; the second, a course on "The History of Literature, or the Successive Periods of European Culture," delivered in Edward-street, Portman-square, in 1838; the third, a course on "the Revolutions of Modern Europe," delivered in 1839; and the fourth, a course on "Heroes, Hero-worship, and the Heroic in History," delivered in 1840. This last course alone was published; and it became more immediately popular than any of the works which had preceded it. It was followed, in 1843, by "Past and Present," a work contrasting, in a historico-philosophical spirit, English society of the middle ages with English society in our own day; and this again, in 1845, by "Oliver Cromwell's Letters and Speeches, with elucidations and a connecting narrative;" such being the unpretending form which a work, originally intended to be a history of Cromwell and his times, ultimately assumed. By the year 1849, this work had reached a third edition. In 1850, appeared the "Latter-Day Pamphlets," in which, more than in any previous publication, the author spoke out in the character of a social and political censor of his own age. From their very nature, as stern denunciations of what the author considered contemporary fallacies, wrongs, and hypocrisies, these pamphlets produced a storm of critical indignation against Mr. Carlyle, which was still raging, when, in 1851, he gave to the world his "Life of John Sterling." While we write (April, 1856) this, with the exception of some papers in periodicals, is the last publication that has proceeded from his pen; but at the present the British public are anxiously expecting a "History of the Life and Times of Frederick the Great," in which he is known to have been long engaged. A collection of some of the most striking opinions, sentiments, and descriptions, contained in all his works hitherto written, has been published in a single volume, entitled, "Passages selected from the Writings of Thomas Carlyle," (1855,) from the memoir prefixed to which, by the editor, Mr. Thomas Ballantyne, we have derived most of the facts for this notice.

An appreciation of Mr. Carlyle's genius and of his influence on British thought and literature, is not to be looked for here, and indeed is hardly possible in the still raging conflict of opinions— one might even say, passions and parties—respecting him. The following remarks, however, by one of his critics, seems to us to express what all must admit to be the literal truth:—"It is nearly half a generation since Mr. Carlyle became an intellectual power in this country; and certainly rarely, if ever, in the history of literature, has such a phenomenon been witnessed as that of his influence. Throughout the whole atmosphere of this island his spirit has diffused itself, so that there is, probably, not an educated man under forty years of age, from Caithness to Cornwall, that can honestly say that he has not been more or less affected by it. Not to speak of his express imitators, one can hardly take up a book or a periodical, without finding some expression or some mode of thinking that bears the mint-mark of his genius." The same critic notices it as a peculiarity in Mr. Carlyle's literary career, that, whereas most men begin with the vehement and the controversial, and gradually become calm and acquiescent in things as they are, he began as an artist in pure literature, a critic of poetry, song, and the drama, and has ended as a vehement moralist and preacher of social reforms, disdaining the etiquette and even the name of pure literature, and more anxious to rouse than to please. With this development of his views of his own functions as a writer, is connected the development of his literary style, from the quiet and pleasing, though still solid and deep beauty of his earlier writings, to that later and more peculiar, and to many, disagreeable form, which has been nicknamed 'the Carlylese.'

As all the world knows, two volumes of Carlyle's Frederick the Great have recently appeared. We might add, from personal acquaintance, many anecdotes, but we have learned, during a long residence abroad, to respect the hospitality that we have enjoyed.

O. W. Wight.
January, 1859.

LIFE OF BURNS.
PART FIRST.

Robert Burns, the national bard of Scotland, was born on the 25th of January, 1759, in a clay-built cottage about two miles south of the town of Ayr. He was the eldest son of William Burnes, or Burness, who, at the period of Robert's birth, was gardener and overseer to a gentleman of small estate; but resided on a few acres of land which he had on lease from another person. The father was a man of strict religious principles, and also distinguished for that penetration and knowledge of mankind which was afterwards so conspicuous in his son. The mother of the poet was likewise a very sagacious woman, and possessed an inexhaustible store of ballads and legendary tales, with which she nourished the infant imagination of him whose own productions were destined to excel them all.

These worthy individuals labored diligently for the support of an increasing family; nor, in the midst of harassing struggles did they neglect the mental improvement of their offspring; a characteristic of Scottish parents, even under the most depressing circumstances. In his sixth year, Robert was put under the tuition of one Campbell, and subsequently under Mr. John Murdoch, a very faithful and pains-taking teacher. With this individual he remained for a few years, and was accurately instructed in the first principles of composition. The poet and his brother Gilbert were the aptest pupils in the school, and were generally at the head of the class. Mr. Murdoch, in afterwards recording the impressions which the two brothers made on him, says: "Gilbert always appeared to me to possess a more lively imagination, and to be more of the wit, than Robert. I attempted to teach them a little church music. Here they were left far behind by all the rest of the school. Robert's ear, in particular, was remarkably dull, and his voice untunable. It was long before I could get them to distinguish one tune from another. Robert's countenance was generally grave, and expressive of a serious, contemplative, and thoughtful mind. Gilbert's face said, *Mirth, with thee I mean to live*; and certainly, if any person who knew the two boys had been asked which of them was the most likely to court the muses, he would never have guessed that *Robert* had a propensity of that kind."

Besides the tuition of Mr. Murdoch, Burns received instructions from his father in writing and arithmetic. Under their joint care, he made rapid progress, and was remarkable for the ease with which he committed devotional poetry to memory. The following extract from his letter to Dr. Moore, in 1787, is interesting, from the light which it throws upon his progress as a scholar, and on the formation of his character as a poet:—"At those years," says he, "I was by no means a favorite with anybody. I was a good deal noted for a retentive memory, a stubborn, sturdy something in my disposition, and an enthusiastic idiot piety. I say idiot piety, because I was then but a child. Though it cost the schoolmaster some thrashings, I made an excellent scholar; and by the time I was ten or eleven years of age, I was a critic in substantives, verbs, and particles. In my infant and boyish days, too, I owed much to an old woman who resided in the family, remarkable for her ignorance, credulity, and superstition. She had, I suppose, the largest collection in the country, of tales and songs, concerning devils, ghosts, fairies, brownies, witches, warlocks, spunkies, kelpies, elf-candles, dead-lights, wraiths, apparitions, cantrips, giants, enchanted towers, dragons, and other trumpery. This cultivated the latent seeds of poetry; but had so strong an effect upon my imagination, that to this hour, in my nocturnal rambles, I sometimes keep a sharp look-out in suspicious places; and though nobody can be more skeptical than I am in such matters, yet it often takes an effort of philosophy to shake off these idle terrors. The earliest composition that I recollect taking pleasure in, was, *The Vision of Mirza*, and a hymn of Addison's, beginning, *"How are thy servants blest, O Lord!"* I particularly remember one-half stanza, which was music to my boyish ear:

"For though on dreadful whirls we hung High on the broken wave."

15

I met with these pieces in *Mason's English Collection*, one of my school-books. The first two books I ever read in private, and which gave me more pleasure than any two books I ever read since, were, *The Life of Hannibal*, and *The History of Sir William Wallace*. Hannibal gave my young ideas such a turn, that I used to strut in raptures up and down after the recruiting drum and bagpipe, and wish myself tall enough to be a soldier; while the story of Wallace poured a tide of Scottish prejudice into my veins, which will boil along there till the flood-gates of life shut in eternal rest."

Mr. Murdoch's removal from Mount Oliphant deprived Burns of his instructions; but they were still continued by the father of the bard. About the age of fourteen, he was sent to school every alternate week for the improvement of his writing. In the mean while, he was busily employed upon the operations of the farm; and, at the age of fifteen, was considered as the principal laborer upon it. About a year after this he gained three weeks of respite, which he spent with his old tutor, Murdoch, at Ayr, in revising the English grammar, and in studying the French language, in which he made uncommon progress. Ere his sixteenth year elapsed, he had considerably extended his reading. The vicinity of Mount Oliphant to Ayr afforded him facilities for gratifying what had now become a passion. Among the books which he had perused were some plays of Shakspeare, Pope, the works of Allan Ramsay, and a collection of songs, which constituted his *vade mecum*. "I pored over them," says he, "driving my cart or walking to labor, song by song, verse by verse, carefully noticing the true, tender or sublime, from affectation and fustian." So early did he evince his attachment to the lyric muse, in which he was destined to surpass all who have gone before or succeeded him.

At this period the family removed to Lochlea, in the parish of Tarbolton. Some time before, however, he had made his first attempt in poetry. It was a song addressed to a rural beauty, about his own age, and though possessing no great merit as a whole, it contains some lines and ideas which would have done honor to him at any age. After the removal to Lochlea, his literary zeal slackened, for he was thus cut off from those acquaintances whose conversation stimulated his powers, and whose kindness supplied him with books. For about three years after this period, he was busily employed upon the farm, but at intervals he paid his addresses to the poetic muse, and with no common success. The summer of his nineteenth year was spent in the study of mensuration, surveying, etc., at a small sea-port town, a good distance from home. He returned to his father's considerably improved. "My reading," says he, "was enlarged with the very important addition of Thomson's and Shenstone's works. I had seen human nature in a new phasis; and I engaged several of my school-fellows to keep up a literary correspondence with me. This improved me in composition. I had met with a collection of letters by the wits of Queen Anne's reign, and I pored over them most devoutly; I kept copies of any of my own letters that pleased me, and a comparison between them and the composition of most of my correspondents flattered my vanity. I carried this whim so far, that though I had not three farthings' worth of business in the world, yet almost every post brought me as many letters as if I had been a broad, plodding son of day-book and ledger."

His mind, peculiarly susceptible of tender impressions, was continually the slave of some rustic charmer. In the "heat and whirlwind of his love," he generally found relief in poetry, by which, as by a safety-valve, his turbulent passions were allowed to have vent. He formed the resolution of entering the matrimonial state; but his circumscribed means of subsistence as a farmer preventing his taking that step, he resolved on becoming a flax-dresser, for which purpose he removed to the town of Irvine, in 1781. The speculation turned out unsuccessful; for the shop, catching fire, was burnt, and the poet returned to his father without a sixpence. During his stay at Irvine he had met with Ferguson's poems. This circumstance was of some importance to Burns, for it roused his poetic powers from the torpor into which they had fallen, and in a great measure finally determined the *Scottish* character of his poetry. He here also contracted some

17

friendships, which he himself says did him mischief; and, by his brother Gilbert's account, from this date there was a serious change in his conduct. The venerable and excellent parent of the poet died soon after his son's return. The support of the family now devolving upon Burns, in conjunction with his brother he took a sub-lease of the farm of Mossgiel, in the parish of Mauchline. The four years which he resided upon this farm were the most important of his life. It was here he felt that nature had designed him for a poet; and here, accordingly, his genius began to develop its energies in those strains which will make his name familiar to all future times, the admiration of every civilized country, and the glory and boast of his own.

The vigor of Burns's understanding, and the keenness of his wit, as displayed more particularly at masonic meetings and debating clubs, of which he formed one at Mauchline, began to spread his fame as a man of uncommon endowments. He now could number as his acquaintance several clergymen, and also some gentlemen of substance; amongst whom was Mr. Gavin Hamilton, writer in Mauchline, one of his earliest patrons. One circumstance more than any other contributed to increase his notoriety. "Polemical divinity," says he to Dr. Moore in 1787, "about this time was putting the country half mad; and I, ambitious of shining in conversation-parties on Sundays, at funerals, etc., used to puzzle Calvinism with so much heat and indiscretion, that I raised a hue-and-cry of heresy against me, which has not ceased to this hour." The farm which he possessed belonged to the Earl of Loudon, but the brothers held it in sub-lease from Mr. Hamilton. This gentleman was at open feud with one of the ministers of Mauchline, who was a rigid Calvinist. Mr. Hamilton maintained opposite tenets; and it is not matter of surprise that the young farmer should have espoused his cause, and brought all the resources of his genius to bear upon it. The result was *The Holy Fair, The Ordination, Holy Willie's Prayer,* and other satires, as much distinguished for their coarse severity and bitterness, as for their genius.

The applause which greeted these pieces emboldened the poet, and encouraged him to proceed. In his life, by his brother Gilbert, a very interesting account is given of the occasions which gave rise to the poems, and the chronological order in which they were produced. The exquisite pathos and humor, the strong manly sense, the masterly command of felicitous language, the graphic power of delineating scenery, manners, and incidents, which appear so conspicuously in his various poems, could not fail to call forth the admiration of those who were favored with a perusal of them. But the clouds of misfortune were gathering darkly above the head of him who was thus giving delight to a large and widening circle of friends. The farm of Mossgiel proved a losing concern; and an amour with Miss Jane Armour, afterwards Mrs. Burns, had assumed so serious an aspect, that he at first resolved to fly from the scene of his disgrace and misery. One trait of his character, however, must be mentioned. Before taking any steps for his departure, he met Miss Armour by appointment, and gave into her hands a written acknowledgment of marriage, which, when produced by a person in her situation, is, according to the Scots' law, to be accepted as legal evidence of an *irregular* marriage having really taken place. This the lady burned, at the persuasion of her father, who was adverse to a marriage; and Burns, thus wounded in the two most powerful feelings of his mind, his love and pride, was driven almost to insanity. Jamaica was his destination; but as he did not possess the money necessary to defray the expense of his passage out, he resolved to publish some of his best poems, in order to raise the requisite sum. These views were warmly promoted by some of his more opulent friends; and a sufficiency of subscribers having been procured, one of the finest volumes of poetry that ever appeared in the world issued from the provincial press of Kilmarnock.

It is hardly possible to imagine with what eager admiration and delight they were every where received. They possessed in an eminent degree all those qualities which invariably contribute to render any literary work quickly and permanently popular. They were written in a phraseology of which all the powers were universally felt, and which being at once antique, familiar, and now rarely written, was therefore fitted to serve all the dignified and picturesque uses of poetry, without making it unintelligible. The imagery and the sentiments were at once natural, impressive, and interesting. Those topics of satire and scandal in which the rustic delights; that humorous imitation of character, and that witty association of ideas, familiar and striking, yet not naturally allied to one another, which has force to shake his sides with laughter; those fancies of superstition, at which one still wonders and trembles; those affecting sentiments and images of true religion, which are at once dear and awful to the heart; were all represented by Burns with the magical power of true poetry. Old and young, high and low, grave and gay, learned and ignorant, all were alike surprised and transported.

In the mean time, a few copies of these fascinating poems found their way to Edinburgh, and having been read to Dr. Blacklock, obtained his warmest approbation; and he advised the author to repair to Edinburgh. Burns lost no time in complying with this request; and accordingly, towards the end of the year 1786, he set out for the capitol, where he was received by Dr. Blacklock with the most flattering kindness, and introduced to every person of taste among that excellent man's friends. Multitudes now vied with each other in patronizing the rustic poet. Those who possessed at once true taste and ardent philanthropy were soon united in his praise; those who were disposed to favor any good thing belonging to Scotland, purely because it was Scottish, gladly joined the cry; while those who had hearts and understandings to be charmed without knowing why, when they saw their native customs, manners, and language, made the subjects and the materials of poesy, could not suppress that impulse of feeling which struggled to declare itself in favor of Burns.

Thus did Burns, ere he had been many weeks in Edinburgh, find himself the object of universal curiosity, favor, admiration, and fondness. He was sought after, courted with attentions the most respectful and assiduous, feasted, flattered, caressed, and treated by all ranks as the great boast of his country, whom it was scarcely possible to honor and reward in a degree equal to his merits.

A new edition of his poems was called for; and the public mind was directed to the subject by Henry Mackenzie, who dedicated a paper in the *Lounger* to a commendatory notice of the poet. This circumstance will ever be remembered to the honor of that polished writer, not only for the warmth of the eulogy he bestowed, but because it was the first printed acknowledgment which had been made to the genius of Burns. The copyright was sold to Creech for £100; but the friends of the poet advised him to forward a subscription. The patronage of the Caledonian Hunt, a very influential body, was obtained. The list of subscribers rapidly rose to 1500, many gentlemen paying a great deal more than the price of the volume; and it was supposed that the poet derived from the subscription and the sale of his copyright a clear profit of at least £700.

The conversation of Burns, according to the testimony of all the eminent men who heard him, was even more wonderful than his poetry. He affected no soft air nor graceful motions of politeness, which might have ill accorded with the rustic plainness of his native manners. Conscious superiority of mind taught him to associate with the great, the learned, and the gay, without being overawed into any such bashfulness as might have rendered him confused in thought, or hesitating in elocution. He possessed withal an extraordinary share of plain common sense, or mother-wit, which prevented him from obtruding upon persons, of whatever rank, with whom he was admitted to converse, any of those effusions of vanity, envy, or self-conceit, in which authors who have lived remote from the general practice of life, and whose minds have been almost exclusively confined to contemplate their own studies and their own works, are but too prone to indulge. In conversation, he displayed a sort of intuitive quickness and rectitude of judgment, upon every subject that arose. The sensibility of his heart, and the vivacity of his fancy, gave a rich coloring to whatever opinions he was disposed to advance; and his language was thus not less happy in conversation than in his writings. Hence those who had met and conversed with him once, were pleased to meet and to converse with him again and again.

For some time he associated only with the virtuous, the learned, and the wise, and the purity of his morals remained uncontaminated. But unfortunately he fell, as others have fallen in similar circumstances. He suffered himself to be surrounded by persons who were proud to tell that they had been in company with Burns, and had seen Burns as loose and as foolish as themselves. He now also began to contract something of arrogance in conversation. Accustomed to be among his associates what is vulgarly but expressively called "the cock of the company," he could scarcely refrain from indulging in a similar freedom and dictatorial decision of talk, even in the presence of persons who could less patiently endure presumption.

After remaining some months in the Scottish metropolis, basking in the noontide sun of a popularity which, as Dugald Stewart well remarks, would have turned any head but his own, he formed a resolution of returning to the shades whence he had emerged, but not before he had perambulated the southern border. On the 6th of May, 1787, he set out on his journey, and, visiting all that appeared interesting on the north of the Tweed, proceeded to Newcastle and other places on the English side. He returned in about two months to his family at Mauchline; but in a short period he again set out on an excursion to the north, where he was most flatteringly received by all the great families. On his return to Mossgiel he completed his marriage with Miss Armour. He then concluded a bargain with Mr. Miller of Dalswinton, for a lease of the farm of Elliesland, on advantageous terms.

Burns entered on possession of this farm at Whit-Sunday, 1788. He had formerly applied with success for an excise commission, and during six weeks of this year, he had to attend to the business of that profession at Ayr. His life for some time was thus wandering and unsettled; and Dr. Currie mentions this as one of his chief misfortunes. Mrs. Burns came home to him towards the end of the year, and the poet was accustomed to say that the happiest period of his life was the first winter spent in Elliesland. The neighboring farmers and gentlemen, pleased to obtain for a neighbor the poet by whose works they had been delighted, kindly sought his company, and invited him to their houses. Burns, however, found an inexpressible charm in sitting down beside his wife, at his own fireside; in wandering over his own grounds; in once more putting his hand to the spade and the plough; in farming his enclosures, and managing his cattle. For some months he felt almost all that felicity which fancy had taught him to expect in his new situation. He had been for a time idle; but his muscles were not yet unbraced for rural toil. He now seemed to find a joy in being the husband of the mistress of his affections, and in seeing himself the father of children such as promised to attach him for ever to that modest, humble, and domestic life, in which alone he could hope to be permanently happy. Even his engagements in the service of excise did not, at first, threaten either to contaminate the poet or to ruin the farmer.

From various causes, the farming speculation did not succeed. Indeed, from the time he obtained a situation under government, he gradually began to sink the farmer in the exciseman. Occasionally he assisted in the rustic occupations of Elliesland, but for the most part he was engaged in very different pursuits. In his professional perambulations over the moors of Dumfries-shire he had to encounter temptations which a mind and temperament like his found it difficult to resist. His immortal works had made him universally known and enthusiastically admired; and accordingly he was a welcome guest at every house, from the most princely mansion to the lowest country inn. In the latter he was too frequently to be found as the presiding genius, and master of the orgies. However, he still continued at intervals to cultivate the muse; and, besides a variety of other pieces, he produced at this period the inimitable poem of Tam O'Shanter. Johnson's Miscellany was also indebted to him for the finest of its lyrics. One pleasing trait of his character must not be overlooked. He superintended the formation of a subscription library in the parish, and took the whole management of it upon himself. These institutions, though common now, were not so short at the period of which we write; and it should never be forgotten that Burns was amongst the first, if not the very first, of their founders in the rural districts of southern Scotland.

Towards the close of 1791 he finally abandoned his farm; and obtaining an appointment to the Dumfries division of excise, he repaired to that town on a salary of £70 per annum. All his principal biographers concur in stating that after settling in Dumfries his moral career was downwards. Heron, who had some acquaintance with the matter, says, "His dissipation became still more deeply habitual; he was here more exposed than in the country to be solicited to share the revels of the dissolute and the idle; foolish young men flocked eagerly about him, and from time to time pressed him to drink with them, that they might enjoy his wit. The Caledonia Club, too, and the Dumfries-shire and Galloway Hunt, had occasional meetings in Dumfries after Burns went to reside there: and the poet was of course invited to share their conviviality, and hesitated not to accept the invitation. In the intervals between his different fits of intemperance, he suffered the keenest anguish of remorse, and horribly afflictive foresight. His Jane behaved with a degree of conjugal and maternal tenderness and prudence, which made him feel more bitterly the evil of his misconduct, although they could not reclaim him."

This is a dark picture—perhaps too dark. The Rev. Mr. Gray, who, as the teacher of his son, was intimately acquainted with Burns, and had frequent opportunities of judging of his general character and deportment, gives a more amiable portrait of the bard. Being an eye-witness, the testimony of this gentleman must be allowed to have some weight. "The truth is," says he, "Burns was seldom *intoxicated*. The drunkard soon becomes besotted, and is shunned even by the convivial. Had he been so, he could not have long continued the idol of every party." This is strong reasoning; and he goes on to mention other circumstances which seem to confirm the truth of his position. In balancing these two statements, a juster estimate of the moral deportment of Burns may be formed.

In the year 1792 party politics ran to a great height in Scotland, and the liberal and independent spirit of Burns did certainly betray him into some indiscretions. A general opinion prevails, that he so far lost the good graces of his superiors by his conduct, as to consider all prospects of future promotion as hopeless. But this appears not to have been the case; and the fact that he acted as supervisor before his death is a strong proof to the contrary. Of his political verses, few have as yet been published. But in these he warmly espoused the cause of the Whigs, which kept up the spleen of the other party, already sufficiently provoked; and this may in some measure account for the bitterness with which his own character was attacked.

Whatever opinion may be formed of the extent of his dissipation in Dumfries, one fact is unquestionable, that his powers remained unimpaired to the last; it was there he produced his finest lyrics, and they are the finest, as well as the purest, that ever delighted mankind. Besides Johnson's *Museum*, in which he took an interest to the last, and to which he contributed most extensively, he formed a connection with Mr. George Thomson, of Edinburgh. This gentleman had conceived the laudable design of collecting the national melodies of Scotland, with accompaniments by the most eminent composers, and poetry by the best writers, in addition to those words which were originally attached to them. From the multitude of songs which Burns wrote, from the year 1792 till the commencement of his illness, it is evident that few days could have passed without his producing some stanzas for the work. The following passage from his correspondence, which was also most extensive, proves that his songs were not hurriedly got up, but composed with the utmost care and attention. "Until I am complete master of a tune in my own singing, such as it is," says he, "I can never compose for it. My way is this: I consider the poetic sentiment correspondent to my idea of the musical expression—then choose my theme— compose one stanza. When that is composed, which is generally the most difficult part of the business, I walk out—sit down now and then—look out for objects in nature round me that are in unison or harmony with the cogitations of my fancy, and workings of my bosom—humming every now and then the air, with the verses I have framed. When I feel my muse beginning to jade, I retire to the solitary fireside of my study, and there commit my effusions to paper; swinging at intervals on the hind legs of my elbow-chair, by way of calling forth my own critical strictures, as my pen goes. Seriously, this, at home, is almost invariably my way." This is not only interesting for the light which it throws upon his method of composition, but it proves that conviviality had not as yet greater charms for him than the muse.

From his youth Burns had exhibited ominous symptoms of a radical disorder in his constitution. A palpitation of the heart, and a derangement of the digestive organs, were conspicuous. These were, doubtless, increased by his indulgences, which became more frequent as he drew towards the close of his career. In the autumn of 1795 he lost an only daughter, which was a severe blow to him. Soon afterwards he was seized with a rheumatic fever; and "long the die spun doubtful," says he, in a letter to his faithful friend Mrs. Dunlap, "until, after many weeks of a sick bed, it seems to have turned up life, and I am beginning to crawl across my room." The cloud behind which his sun was destined to be eclipsed at noon had begun to darken above him. Before he had completely recovered, he had the imprudence to join a festive circle; and, on his return from it, he caught a cold, which brought back his trouble upon him with redoubled severity. Sea-bathing was had recourse to, but with no ultimate success. He lingered until the 21st of July, 1796, when he expired. The interest which the death of Burns excited was intense. All differences were forgotten; his genius only was thought of. On the 26th of the same month he was conveyed to the grave, followed by about ten thousand individuals of all ranks, many of whom had come from distant parts of the country to witness the solemnity. He was interred with military honors by the Dumfries volunteers, to which body he had belonged.

Thus, at the age of thirty-seven, an age when the mental powers of man have scarcely reached their climax, died Robert Burns, one of the greatest poets whom his country has produced. It is unnecessary to enter into any lengthened analysis of his poetry or character. His works are universally known and admired, and criticism has been drawn to the dregs upon the subject; and that, too, by the greatest masters who have appeared since his death,—no mean test of the great merits of his writings. He excels equally in touching the heart by the exquisiteness of his pathos, and exciting the risible faculties by the breadth of his humor. His lyre had many strings, and he had equal command over them all; striking each, and frequently in chords, with the skill and power of a master. That his satire sometimes degenerates into coarse invective, can not be denied; but where personality is not permitted to interfere, his poems of this description may take their place beside any thing of the kind which has ever been produced, without being disgraced by the comparison. It is unnecessary to re-echo the praises of his best pieces, as there is no epithet of admiration which has not been bestowed upon them. Those who had best opportunities of judging, are of opinion that his works, stamped as they are with the impress of sovereign genius, fall short of the powers he possessed. It is therefore to be lamented that he undertook no great work of fiction or invention. Had circumstances permitted, he would probably have done so; but his excise duties, and without doubt his own follies, prevented him. His passions were strong, and his capacity of enjoyment corresponded with them. These continually precipitated him into the variety of pleasure, where alone they could be gratified; and the reaction consequent upon such indulgences (for he possessed the finest discrimination between right and wrong) threw him into low spirits, to which he was also constitutionally liable. His mind, being thus never for any length of time in an equable tone, could scarcely pursue with steady regularity a work of any length. His moral aberrations, as detailed by some of his biographers, have been exaggerated, as already noticed. This has been proved by the testimony of many witnesses, from whose authority there can be no appeal; for they had the best opportunities of judging. In fine, it may be doubted whether he has not, by his writings, exercised a greater power over the minds of men, and the general system of life, than has been exercised by any other modern poet. A complete edition of his works, in four vols. 8vo., with a life, was published by Dr. Currie of Liverpool, for the benefit of his family, to whom it realized a handsome sum. Editions have been since multiplied beyond number; and several excellent biographies of the poet have been published, particularly that by Mr. Lockhart.

LIFE OF BURNS.[1]

PART SECOND.

In the modern arrangements of society, it is no uncommon thing that a man of genius must, like Butler, "ask for bread and receive a stone;" for, in spite of our grand maxim of supply and demand, it is by no means the highest excellence that men are most forward to recognize. The inventor of a spinning-jenny is pretty sure of his reward in his own day; but the writer of a true poem, like the apostle of a true religion, is nearly as sure of the contrary. We do not know whether it is not an aggravation of the injustice, that there is generally a posthumous retribution. Robert Burns, in the course of nature, might yet have been living; but his short life was spent in toil and penury; and he died, in the prime of his manhood, miserable and neglected; and yet already a brave mausoleum shines over his dust, and more than one splendid monument has been reared in other places to his fame: the street where he languished in poverty is called by his name; the highest personages in our literature have been proud to appear as his commentators and admirers, and here is the *sixth* narrative of his *Life*, that has been given to the world!

Mr. Lockhart thinks it necessary to apologize for this new attempt on such a subject: but his readers, we believe, will readily acquit him; or, at worst, will censure only the performance of his task, not the choice of it. The character of Burns, indeed, is a theme that cannot easily become either trite or exhausted; and will probably gain rather than lose in its dimensions by the distance to which it is removed by Time. No man, it has been said, is a hero to his valet: and this is probably true; but the fault is at least as likely to be the valet's as the hero's: For it is certain, that to the vulgar eye few things are wonderful that are not distant. It is difficult for men to believe that the man, the mere man whom they see, nay, perhaps, painfully feel, toiling at their side through

---

[1] A review of the Life of Robert Burns. By J. G. Lockhart, LL. B. Edinburgh, 1828.

the poor jostlings of existence, can be made of finer clay than themselves. Suppose that some dining acquaintance of Sir Thomas Lucy's, and neighbour of John a Combe's, had snatched an hour or two from the preservation of his game, and written us a Life of Shakspeare! What dissertations should we not have had,—not on *Hamlet* and *The Tempest*, but on the wool-trade and deer-stealing, and the libel and vagrant laws! and how the Poacher became a Player; and how Sir Thomas and Mr. John had Christian bowels, and did not push him to extremities! In like manner, we believe, with respect to Burns, that till the companions of his pilgrimage, the honourable Excise Commissioners, and the Gentlemen of the Caledonian Hunt, and the Dumfries Aristocracy, and all the Squires and Earls, equally with the Ayr Writers, and the New and Old Light Clergy, whom he had to do with, shall have become invisible in the darkness of the Past, or visible only by light borrowed from *his* juxtaposition, it will be difficult to measure him by any true standard, or to estimate what he really was and did, in the eighteenth century, for his country and the world. It will be difficult, we say; but still a fare problem for literary historians; and repeated attempts will give us repeated approximations.

His former biographers have done something, no doubt, but by no means a great deal, to assist us. Dr. Currie and Mr. Walker, the principal of these writers, have both, we think, mistaken one essentially important thing:—Their own and the world's true relation to their author, and the style in which it became such men to think and to speak of such a man. Dr. Currie loved the poet truly; more perhaps than he avowed to his readers, or even to himself; yet he everywhere introduces him with a certain patronizing, apologetic air; as if the polite public might think it strange and half unwarrantable that he, a man of science, a scholar, and gentleman, should do such honour to a rustic. In all this, however, we readily admit that his fault was not want of love, but weakness of faith; and regret that the first and kindest of all our poet's biographers should not have seen farther, or believed more boldly what he saw. Mr. Walker offends more deeply in the same kind: and both err alike in presenting us with a detached catalogue of his several supposed attributes, virtues, and vices, instead of a delineation of the resulting character as a living unity. This, however, is not painting a portrait; but gauging the length and breadth of the several features, and jotting down their dimensions in arithmetical ciphers. Nay, it is not so much as this: for we are yet to learn by what arts or instruments the mind *could* be so measured and gauged.

Mr. Lockhart, we are happy to say, has avoided both these errors. He uniformly treats Burns as the high and remarkable man the public voice has now pronounced him to be: and in delineating him, he has avoided the method of separate generalities, and rather sought for characteristic incidents, habits, actions, sayings; in a word, for aspects which exhibit the whole man, as he looked and lived among his fellows. The book accordingly, with all its deficiencies, gives more insight, we think, into the true character of Burns, than any prior biography; though, being written on the very popular and condensed scheme of an article for *Constable's Miscellany*, it has less depth than we could have wished and expected from a writer of such power, and contains rather more, and more multifarious, quotations, than belong of right to an original production. Indeed, Mr. Lockhart's own writing is generally so good, so clear, direct, and nervous, that we seldom wish to see it making place for another man's. However, the spirit of the work is throughout candid, tolerant, and anxiously conciliating; compliments and praises are liberally distributed, on all hands, to great and small; and, as Mr. Morris Birkbeck observes of the society in the backwoods of America, "the courtesies of polite life are never lost sight of for a moment." But there are better things than these in the volume; and we can safely testify, not only that it is easily and pleasantly read a first time, but may even be without difficulty read again.

Nevertheless, we are far from thinking that the problem of Burns's Biography has yet been adequately solved. We do not allude so much to deficiency of facts or documents,—though of these we are still every day receiving some fresh accession,—as to the limited and imperfect application of them to the great end of Biography. Our notions upon this subject may perhaps appear extravagant; but if an individual is really of consequence enough to have his life and character recorded for public remembrance, we have always been of opinion, that the public ought to be made acquainted with all the inward springs and relations of his character. How did the world and man's life, from his particular position, represent themselves to his mind? How did coexisting circumstances modify him from without? how did he modify these from within? With what endeavors and what efficacy rule over them? with what resistance and what suffering sink under them? In one word, what and how produced was the effect of society on him? what and how produced was his effect on society? He who should answer these questions, in regard to any individual, would, as we believe, furnish a model of perfection in biography. Few individuals, indeed, can deserve such a study; and many *lives* will be written, and, for the gratification of innocent curiosity, ought to be written, and read, and forgotten, which are not in this sense *biographies*. But Burns, if we mistake not, is one of these few individuals; and such a study, at least with such a result, he has not yet obtained. Our own contributions to it, we are aware, can be but scanty and feeble; but we offer them with goodwill, and trust they may meet with acceptance from those for whom they are intended.

Burns first came upon the world as a prodigy; and was, in that character, entertained by it, in the usual fashion, with loud, vague, tumultuous wonder, speedily subsiding into censure and neglect; till his early and most mournful death again awakened an enthusiasm for him, which, especially as there was now nothing to be done, and much to be spoken, has prolonged itself even to our own time. It is true, the "nine days" have long since elapsed; and the very continuance of this clamor proves that Burns was no vulgar wonder. Accordingly, even in sober judgments, where, as years passed by, he has come to rest more and more exclusively on his own intrinsic merits, and may now be well nigh shorn of that casual radiance, he appears not only as a true British poet, but as one of the most considerable British men of the eighteenth century. Let it not be objected that he did little: he did much, if we consider where and how. If the work performed was small, we must remember that he had his very materials to discover; for the metal he worked in lay hid under the desert, where no eye but his had guessed its existence; and we may almost say, that with his own hand he had to construct the tools for fashioning it. For he found himself in deepest obscurity, without help, without instruction, without model; or with models only of the meanest sort. An educated man stands, as it were, in the midst of a boundless arsenal and magazine, filled with all the weapons and engines which man's skill has been able to devise from the earliest time; and he works, accordingly, with a strength borrowed from all past ages. How different is *his* state who stands on the outside of that storehouse, and feels that its gates must be stormed, or remain for ever shut against him? His means are the commonest and rudest; the mere work done is no measure of his strength. A dwarf behind his steam engine may remove mountains; but no dwarf will hew them down with the pick-axe; and he must be a Titan that hurls them abroad with his arms.

It is in this last shape that Burns presents himself. Born in an age the most prosaic Britain had yet seen, and in a condition the most disadvantageous, where his mind, if it accomplished aught, must accomplish it under the pressure of continual bodily toil, nay, of penury and desponding apprehension of the worst evils, and with no furtherance but such knowledge as dwells in a poor man's hut, and the rhymes of a Ferguson or Ramsay for his standard of beauty, he sinks not under all these impediments. Through the fogs and darkness of that obscure region, his eagle eye discerns the true relations of the world and human life; he grows into intellectual strength, and trains himself into intellectual expertness. Impelled by the irrepressible movement of his inward spirit, he struggles forward into the general view, and with haughty modesty lays down before us, as the fruit of his labor, a gift, which Time has now pronounced imperishable. Add to all this, that his darksome, drudging childhood and youth was by far the kindliest era of his whole life; and that he died in his thirty-seventh year; and then ask if it be strange that his poems are imperfect, and of small extent, or that his genius attained no mastery in its art? Alas, his Sun shone as through a tropical tornado; and the pale Shadow of Death eclipsed it at noon! Shrouded in such baleful vapors, the genius of Burns was never seen in clear azure splendor, enlightening the world. But some beams from it did, by fits, pierce through; and it tinted those clouds with rainbow and orient colors into a glory and stern grandeur, which men silently gazed on with wonder and tears!

We are anxious not to exaggerate; for it is exposition rather than admiration that our readers require of us here; and yet to avoid some tendency to that side is no easy matter. We love Burns, and we pity him; and love and pity are prone to magnify. Criticism, it is sometimes thought, should be a cold business; we are not so sure of this; but, at all events, our concern with Burns is not exclusively that of critics. True and genial as his poetry must appear, it is not chiefly as a poet, but as a man, that he interests and affects us. He was often advised to write a tragedy: time and means were not lent him for this; but through life he enacted a tragedy, and one of the deepest. We question whether the world has since witnessed so utterly sad a scene; whether Napoleon himself, left to brawl with Sir Hudson Lowe, and perish on his rock, "amid the melancholy main," presented to the reflecting mind such a "spectacle of pity and fear," as did this intrinsically nobler, gentler, and perhaps greater soul, wasting itself away in a hopeless struggle with base entanglements, which coiled closer and closer round him, till only death opened him an outlet. Conquerors are a race with whom the world could well dispense; nor can the hard intellect, the unsympathizing loftiness, and high but selfish enthusiasm of such persons, inspire us in general with any affection; at best it may excite amazement; and their fall, like that of a pyramid, will be beheld with a certain sadness and awe. But a true Poet, a man in whose heart resides some effluence of Wisdom, some tone of the "Eternal Melodies," is the most precious gift that can be bestowed on a generation: we see in him a freer, purer, development of whatever is noblest in ourselves; his life is a rich lesson to us, and we mourn his death, as that of a benefactor who loved and taught us.

Such a gift had Nature in her bounty bestowed on us in Robert Burns; but with queen-like indifference she cast it from her hand, like a thing of no moment; and it was defaced and torn asunder, as an idle bauble, before we recognized it. To the ill-starred Burns was given the power of making man's life more venerable, but that of wisely guiding his own was not given. Destiny—for so in our ignorance we must speak,—his faults, the faults of others, proved too hard for him; and that spirit, which might have soared, could it but have walked, soon sank to the dust, its glorious faculties trodden under foot in the blossom, and died, we may almost say, without ever having lived. And so kind and warm a soul; so full of inborn riches, of love to all living and lifeless things! How his heart flows out in sympathy over universal nature; and in her bleakest provinces discerns a beauty and a meaning! The "Daisy" falls not unheeded under his ploughshare; nor the ruined nest of that "wee, cowering, timorous beastie," cast forth, after all its provident pains, to "thole the sleety dribble, and cranreuch cauld." The "hoar visage" of Winter delights him: he dwells with a sad and oft-returning fondness in these scenes of solemn desolation; but the voice of the tempest becomes an anthem to his ears; he loves to walk in the sounding woods, for "it raises his thoughts to *Him that walketh on the wings of the wind.*" A true Poet-soul, for it needs but to be struck, and the sound it yields will be music! But observe him chiefly as he mingles with his brother men. What warm, all-comprehending, fellow-feeling, what trustful, boundless love, what generous exaggeration of the object loved! His rustic friend, his nut-brown maiden, are no longer mean and homely, but a hero and a queen, whom he prizes as the paragons of Earth. The rough scenes of Scottish life, not seen by him in any Arcadian illusion, but in the rude contradiction, in the smoke and soil of a too harsh reality, are still lovely to him: Poverty is indeed his companion, but Love also, and Courage; the simple feelings, the

35

worth, the nobleness, that dwell under the straw roof, are dear and venerable to his heart; and thus over the lowest provinces of man's existence he pours the glory of his own soul; and they rise, in shadow and sunshine, softened and brightened into a beauty which other eyes discern not in the highest. He has a just self-consciousness, which too often degenerates into pride; yet it is a noble pride, for defence, not for offence, no cold, suspicious feeling, but a frank and social one. The peasant Poet bears himself, we might say, like a King in exile; he is cast among the low, and feels himself equal to the highest; yet he claims no rank, that none may be disputed to him. The forward he can repel, the supercilious he can subdue; pretensions of wealth or ancestry are of no avail with him; there is a fire in that dark eye, under which the "insolence of condescension" cannot thrive. In his abasement, in his extreme need, he forgets not for a moment the majesty of Poetry and Manhood. And yet, far as he feels himself above common men, he wanders not apart from them, but mixes warmly in their interests; nay, throws himself into their arms; and, as it were, entreats them to love him. It is moving to see how, in his darkest despondency, this proud being still seeks relief from friendship; unbosoms himself, often to the unworthy; and, amid tears, strains to his glowing heart a heart that knows only the name of friendship. And yet he was "quick to learn;" a man of keen vision, before whom common disguises afforded no concealment. His understanding saw through the hollowness even of accomplished deceivers; but there was a generous credulity in his Heart. And so did our Peasant show himself among us; "a soul like an Æolian harp, in whose strings the vulgar wind, as it passed through them, changed itself into articulate melody." And this was he for whom the world found no fitter business than quarrelling with smugglers and vintners, computing excise dues upon tallow, and gauging ale-barrels! In such toils was that mighty Spirit sorrowfully wasted: and a hundred years may pass on, before another such is given us to waste.

All that remains of Burns, the Writings he has left, seem to us, as we hinted above, no more than a poor mutilated fraction of what was in him; brief, broken glimpses of a genius that could never show itself complete; that wanted all things for completeness; culture, leisure, true effort, nay, even length of life. His poems are, with scarcely any exception, mere occasional effusions, poured forth with little premeditation, expressing, by such means as offered, the passion, opinion, or humor of the hour. Never in one instance was it permitted him to grapple with any subject with the full collection of his strength, to fuse and mould it in the concentrated fire of his genius. To try by the strict rules of Art such imperfect fragments, would be at once unprofitable and unfair. Nevertheless, there is something in these poems, marred and defective as they are, which forbids the most fastidious student of poetry to pass them by. Some sort of enduring quality they must have; for, after fifty years of the wildest vicissitudes in poetic taste, they still continue to be read; nay, are read more and more eagerly, more and more extensively; and this not only by literary virtuosos, and that class upon whom transitory causes operate most strongly, but by all classes, down to the most hard, unlettered, and truly natural class, who read little, and especially no poetry, except because they find pleasure in it. The grounds of so singular and wide a popularity, which extends, in a literal sense, from the palace to the hut, and over all regions where the English tongue is spoken, are well worth inquiring into. After every just deduction, it seems to imply some rare excellence in these works. What is that excellence?

To answer this question will not lead us far. The excellence of Burns is, indeed, among the rarest, whether in poetry or prose; but, at the same time, it is plain and easily recognized: his *Sincerity*, his indisputable air of Truth. Here are no fabulous woes or joys; no hollow fantastic sentimentalities; no wiredrawn refinings, either in thought or feeling: the passion that is traced before us has glowed in a living heart; the opinion he utters has risen in his own understanding, and been a light to his own steps. He does not write from hearsay, but from sight and experience; it is the scenes he has lived and labored amidst, that he describes:

37

those scenes, rude and humble as they are, have kindled beautiful emotions in his soul, noble thoughts, and definite resolves; and he speaks forth what is in him, not from any outward call of vanity or interest, but because his heart is too full to be silent. He speaks it, too, with such melody and modulation as he can; "in homely rustic jingle;" but it is his own, and genuine. This is the grand secret for finding readers and retaining them: let him who would move and convince others, be first moved and convinced himself. Horace's rule, *Si vis me flere*, is applicable in a wider sense than the literal one. To every poet, to every writer, we might say: Be true, if you would be believed. Let a man but speak forth with genuine earnestness the thought, the emotion, the actual condition, of his own heart; and other men, so strangely are we all knit together by the tie of sympathy, must and will give heed to him. In culture, in extent of view, we may stand above the speaker, or below him; but in either case, his words, if they are earnest and sincere, will find some response within us; for in spite of all casual varieties in outward rank, or inward, as face answers to face, so does the heart of man to man.

This may appear a very simple principle, and one which Burns had little merit in discovering. True, the discovery is easy enough: but the practical appliance is not easy; is indeed the fundamental difficulty which all poets have to strive with, and which scarcely one in the hundred ever fairly surmounts. A head too dull to discriminate the true from the false; a heart too dull to love the one at all risks, and to hate the other in spite of all temptations, are alike fatal to a writer. With either, or, as more commonly happens, with both, of these deficiencies, combine a love of distinction, a wish to be original, which is seldom wanting, and we have Affectation, the bane of literature, as Cant, its elder brother, is of morals. How often does the one and the other front us, in poetry, as in life! Great poets themselves are not always free of this vice; nay, it is precisely on a certain sort and degree of greatness that it is most commonly ingrafted. A strong effort after excellence will sometimes solace itself with a mere shadow of success, and he who has much to unfold, will sometimes unfold it imperfectly. Byron, for instance, was no common man: yet if we examine his poetry with this view, we shall find it far enough from faultless. Generally speaking, we should say that it is not true. He refreshes us, not with the divine fountain, but too often with vulgar strong waters, stimulating indeed to the taste, but soon ending in dislike or even nausea. Are his Harolds and Giaours, we would ask, real men, we mean, poetically consistent and conceivable men? Do not these characters, does not the character of their author, which more or less shines through them all, rather appear a thing put on for the occasion; no natural or possible mode of being, but something intended to look much grander than nature? Surely, all these stormful agonies, this volcanic heroism, superhuman contempt, and moody desperation, with so much scowling, and teeth-gnashing, and other sulphurous humors, is more like the brawling of a player in some paltry tragedy, which is to last three hours, than the bearing of a man in the business of life, which is to last threescore and ten years. To our minds, there is a taint of this sort, something which we should call theatrical, false and affected, in every one of these otherwise powerful pieces. Perhaps *Don Juan*, especially the latter parts of it, is the only thing approaching to a *sincere* work, he ever wrote; the only work where he showed himself, in any measure, as he was; and seemed so intent on his subject, as, for moments, to forget himself. Yet Byron hated this vice; we believe, heartily detested it: nay, he had declared formal war against it in words. So difficult is it even for the strongest to make this primary attainment, which might seem the simplest of all: *to read its own consciousness without mistakes*, without errors involuntary or wilful! We recollect no poet of Burns's susceptibility who comes before us from the first, and abides with us to the last, with such a total want of affectation. He is an honest man, and an honest writer. In his successes and his failures, in his greatness and his littleness, he is ever clear, simple, true, and glitters with no lustre but his own. We reckon this to be a great virtue; to be, in fact, the root of most other virtues, literary as well as moral.

It is necessary, however, to mention, that it is to the poetry of Burns that we now allude; to those writings which he had time to meditate, and where no special reason existed to warp his critical feeling, or obstruct his endeavor to fulfil it. Certain of his Letters, and other fractions of prose composition, by no means deserve this praise. Here, doubtless, there is not the same natural truth of style; but on the contrary, something not only stiff, but strained and twisted; a certain high-flown, inflated tone; the stilting emphasis of which contrasts ill with the firmness and rugged simplicity of even his poorest verses. Thus no man, it would appear, is altogether unaffected. Does not Shakspeare himself sometimes premeditate the sheerest bombast! But even with regard to these Letters of Burns, it is but fair to state that he had two excuses. The first was his comparative deficiency in language. Burns, though for most part he writes with singular force, and even gracefulness, is not master of English prose, as he is of Scottish verse; not master of it, we mean, in proportion to the depth and vehemence of his matter. These Letters strike us as the effort of a man to express something which he has no organ fit for expressing. But a second and weightier excuse is to be found in the peculiarity of Burns's social rank. His correspondents are often men whose relation to him he has never accurately ascertained; whom therefore he is either forearming himself against, or else unconsciously flattering, by adopting the style he thinks will please them. At all events, we should remember that these faults, even in his Letters, are not the rule, but the exception. Whenever he writes, as one would ever wish to do, to trusted friends and on real interests, his style becomes simple, vigorous, expressive, sometimes even beautiful. His Letters to Mrs. Dunlop are uniformly excellent.

But we return to his poetry. In addition to its sincerity, it has another peculiar merit, which indeed is but a mode, or perhaps a means, of the foregoing. It displays itself in his choice of subjects, or rather in his indifference as to subjects, and the power he has of making all subjects interesting. The ordinary poet, like the ordinary man, is for ever seeking, in external circumstances, the help which can be found only in himself. In what is familiar and near at hand, he discerns no form or comeliness; home is not poetical but prosaic; it is in some past, distant, conventional world, that poetry resides for him; were he there and not here, were he thus and not so, it would be well with him. Hence our innumerable host of rose-colored novels and iron-mailed epics, with their locality not on the Earth, but somewhere nearer to the Moon. Hence our Virgins of the Sun, and our Knights of the Cross, malicious Saracens in turbans, and copper-colored Chiefs in wampum, and so many other truculent figures from the heroic times or the heroic climates, who on all hands swarm in our poetry. Peace be with them! But yet, as a great moralist proposed preaching to the men of this century, so would we fain preach to the poets, "a sermon on the duty of staying at home." Let them be sure that heroic ages and heroic climates can do little for them. That form of life has attraction for us, less because it is better or nobler than our own, than simply because it is different; and even this attraction must be of the most transient sort. For will not our own age, one day, be an ancient one; and have as quaint a costume as the rest; not contrasted with the rest, therefore, but ranked along with them, in respect of quaintness? Does Homer interest us now, because he wrote of what passed out of his native Greece, and two centuries before he was born; or because he wrote of what passed in God's world, and in the heart of man, which is the same after thirty centuries? Let our poets look to this; is their feeling really finer, truer, and their vision deeper than that of other men, they have nothing to fear, even from the humblest object; is it not so?—they have nothing to hope, but an ephemeral favor, even from the highest.

The poet, we cannot but think, can never have far to seek for a subject; the elements of his art are in him, and around him on every hand; for him the Ideal world is not remote from the Actual, but under it and within it; nay, he is a poet, precisely because he can discern it there. Wherever there is a sky above him, and a world around him, the poet is in his place; for here too is man's existence, with its infinite longings and small acquirings;

its ever-thwarted, ever-renewed endeavors; its unspeakable aspirations, its fears and hopes that wander through Eternity: and all the mystery of brightness and of gloom that it was ever made of, in any age or climate, since man first began to live. Is there not the fifth act of a Tragedy, in every death-bed, though it were a peasant's and a bed of heath? And are wooings and weddings obsolete, that there can be Comedy no longer? Or are men suddenly grown wise, that Laughter must no longer shake his sides, but be cheated of his Farce? Man's life and nature is, as it was, and as it will ever be. But the poet must have an eye to read these things, and a heart to understand them; or they come and pass away before him in vain. He is a *vates*, a seer; a gift of vision has been given him. Has life no meanings for him, which another can not equally decipher? then he is no poet, and Delphi itself will not make him one.

In this respect, Burns, though not perhaps absolutely a great poet, better manifests his capability, better proves the truth of his genius, than if he had, by his own strength, kept the whole Minerva Press going, to the end of his literary course. He shows himself at least a poet of Nature's own making; and Nature, after all, is still the grand agent in making poets. We often hear of this and the other external condition being requisite for the existence of a poet. Sometimes it is a certain sort of training; he must have studied certain things, studied for instance "the elder dramatists," and so learned a poetic language; as if poetry lay in the tongue, not in the heart. At other times we are told, he must be bred in a certain rank, and must be on a confidential footing with the higher classes; because, above all other things, he must see the world. As to seeing the world, we apprehend this will cause him little difficulty, if he have but an eye to see it with. Without eyes, indeed, the task might be hard. But happily every poet is born *in* the world, and sees it, with or against his will, every day and every hour he lives. The mysterious workmanship of man's heart, the true light and the inscrutable darkness of man's destiny, reveal themselves not only in capital cities and crowded saloons, but in every hut and hamlet where men have their abode. Nay, do not the elements of all human virtues, and all human vices—the passions at once of a Borgia and of a Luther, lie written, in stronger or fainter lines, in the consciousness of every individual bosom, that has practised honest self-examination? Truly, this same world may be seen in Mossgiel and Tarbolton, if we look well, as clearly as it ever came to light in Crockford's, or the Tuileries itself.

But sometimes still harder requisitions are laid on the poor aspirant to poetry; for it is hinted that he should have *been born* two centuries ago; inasmuch as poetry, soon after that date, vanished from the earth, and became no longer attainable by men! Such cobweb speculations have, now and then, overhung the field of literature; but they obstruct not the growth of any plant there: the Shakspeare or the Burns, unconsciously, and merely as he walks onward, silently brushes them away. Is not every genius an impossibility till he appear? Why do we call him new and original, if *we* saw where his marble was lying, and what fabric he could rear from it? It is not the material but the workman that is wanting. It is not the dark *place* that hinders, but the dim *eye*. A Scottish peasant's life was the meanest and rudest of all lives, till Burns became a poet in it, and a poet of it; found it a *man's* life, and therefore significant to men. A thousand battle-fields remain unsung; but the *Wounded Hare* has not perished without its memorial; a balm of mercy yet breathes on us from its dumb agonies, because a poet was there. Our *Halloween* had passed and repassed, in rude awe and laughter, since the era of the Druids; but no Theocritus, till Burns, discerned in it the materials of a Scottish Idyl: neither was the *Holy Fair* any *Council of Trent*, or Roman *Jubilee*; but nevertheless, *Superstition* and *Hypocrisy*, and *Fun* having been propitious to him, in this man's hand it became a poem, instinct with satire, and genuine comic life. Let but the true poet be given us, we repeat it, place him where and how you will, and true poetry will not be wanting.

Independently of the essential gift of poetic feeling, as we have now attempted to describe it, a certain rugged sterling worth pervades whatever Burns has written: a virtue, as of green fields and mountain breezes, dwells in his poetry; it is redolent of natural life, and hardy, natural men. There is a decisive strength in him; and yet a sweet native gracefulness: he is tender, and he is vehement, yet without constraint or too visible effort; he melts the heart, or inflames it, with a power which seems habitual and familiar to him. We see in him the gentleness, the trembling pity of a woman, with the deep earnestness, the force and passionate ardor of a hero. Tears lie in him, and consuming fire; as lightning lurks in the drops of the summer cloud. He has a resonance in his bosom for every note of human feeling: the high and the low, the sad, the ludicrous, the joyful, are welcome in their turns to his "lightly-moved and all-conceiving spirit." And observe with what a prompt and eager force he grasps his subject, be it what it may! How he fixes, as it were, the full image of the matter in his eye; full and clear in every lineament; and catches the real type and essence of it, amid a thousand accidents and superficial circumstances, no one of which misleads him! Is it of reason— some truth to be discovered? No sophistry, no vain surface-logic detains him; quick, resolute, unerring, he pierces through into the marrow of the question, and speaks his verdict with an emphasis that can not be forgotten. Is it of description—some visual object to be represented? No poet of any age or nation is more graphic than Burns: the characteristic features disclose themselves to him at a glance; three lines from his hand, and we have a likeness. And, in that rough dialect, in that rude, often awkward, metre, so clear, and definite a likeness! It seems a draughtsman working with a burnt stick; and yet the burin of a Retzsch is not more expressive or exact.

This clearness of sight we may call the foundation of all talent; for in fact, unless we *see* our object, how shall we know how to place or prize it; in our understanding, our imagination, our affections? Yet it is not in itself perhaps a very high excellence; but capable of being united indifferently with the strongest, or with ordinary powers. Homer surpasses all men in this quality: but strangely enough, at no great distance below him are Richardson and Defoe. It belongs, in truth, to what is called a lively mind: and gives no sure indication of the higher endowments that may exist along with it. In all the three cases we have mentioned, it is combined with great garrulity; their descriptions are detailed, ample, and lovingly exact; Homer's fire bursts through, from time to time, as if by accident; but Defoe and Richardson have no fire. Burns, again, is not more distinguished by the clearness than by the impetuous force of his conceptions. Of the strength, the piercing emphasis with which he thought, his emphasis of expression may give an humble but the readiest proof. Who ever uttered sharper sayings than his; words more memorable, now by their burning vehemence, now by their cool vigor and laconic pith? A single phrase depicts a whole subject, a whole scene. Our Scottish forefathers in the battle-field struggled forward, he says, "*red-wat shod*," giving, in this one word, a full vision of horror and carnage, perhaps too frightfully accurate for Art!

In fact, one of the leading features in the mind of Burns is this vigor of his strictly intellectual perceptions. A resolute force is ever visible in his judgments, as in his feelings and volitions. Professor Stewart says of him, with some surprise: "All the faculties of Burns's mind were, as far as I could judge, equally vigorous; and his predilection for poetry was rather the result of his own enthusiastic and impassioned temper, than of a genius exclusively adapted to that species of composition. From his conversation I should have pronounced him to be fitted to excel in whatever walk of ambition he had chosen to exert his abilities." But this, if we mistake not, is at all times the very essence of a truly poetical endowment. Poetry, except in such cases as that of Keats, where the whole consists in extreme sensibility, and a certain vague pervading tunefulness of nature, is no separate faculty, no organ which can be superadded to the rest or disjoined from them; but rather the result of their general harmony and completion. The feelings, the gifts, that exist in the Poet, are those that exist, with more or less development, in every human soul: the imagination, which shudders at the Hell of Dante, is the same faculty, weaker in degree, which called that picture into being. How does the poet speak to all men, with power, but by being still more a man than they? Shakspeare, it has been well observed, in the planning and completing of his tragedies, has shown an Understanding, were it nothing more, which might have governed states, or indited a *Novum Organum*. What Burns's force of understanding may have been, we have less means of judgment: for it dwelt among the humblest objects, never saw philosophy, and never rose, except for short intervals, into the region of great ideas. Nevertheless, sufficient indication remains for us in his works: we discern the brawny movement of a gigantic though untutored strength, and can understand how, in conversation, his quick, sure insight into men and things may, as much as aught else about him, have amazed the best thinkers of his time and country.

But, unless we mistake, the intellectual gift of Burns is fine as well as strong. The more delicate relation of things could not well have escaped his eye, for they were intimately present to his heart. The logic of the senate and the forum is indispensable, but not all-sufficient; nay, perhaps the highest Truth is that which will the most certainly elude it. For this logic works by words, and "the highest," it has been said, "cannot be expressed in words." We are not without tokens of an openness for this higher truth also, of a keen though uncultivated sense for it, having existed in Burns. Mr. Stewart, it will be remembered, "wonders," in the passage above quoted, that Burns had formed some distinct conception of the "doctrine of association." We rather think that far subtiler things than the doctrine of association had from of old been familiar to him. Here for instance:

"We know nothing," thus writes he, "or next to nothing, of the structure of our souls, so we cannot account for those seeming caprices in them, that one should be particularly pleased with this thing, or struck with that, which, on minds of a different cast, makes no extraordinary impression. I have some favorite flowers in spring, among which are the mountain-daisy, the hare-bell, the fox-glove, the wild-brier rose, the budding birch, and the hoary hawthorn, that I view and hang over with particular delight. I never hear the loud solitary whistle of the curlew in a summer noon, or the wild mixing cadence of a troop of gray plover in an autumnal morning, without feeling an elevation of soul like the enthusiasm of devotion or poetry. Tell me, my dear friend, to what can this be owing? Are we a piece of machinery, which, like the Æolian harp, passive, takes the impression of the passing accident; or do these workings argue something within us above the trodden clod? I own myself partial to such proofs of those awful and important realities: a God that made all things, man's immaterial and immortal nature, and a world of weal or wo beyond death and the grave."

Force and fineness of understanding are often spoken of as something different from general force and fineness of nature, as something partly independent of them. The necessities of language probably require this; but in truth these qualities are not distinct and independent: except in special cases, and from special causes, they ever go together. A man of strong understanding is generally a man of strong character; neither is delicacy in the one kind often divided from delicacy in the other. No one, at all events, is ignorant that in the poetry of Burns, keenness of insight keeps pace with keenness of feeling; that his *light* is not more pervading than his *warmth*. He is a man of the most impassioned temper; with passions not strong only, but noble, and of the sort in which great virtues and great poems take their rise. It is reverence, it is Love towards all Nature that inspires him, that opens his eyes to its beauty, and makes heart and voice eloquent in its praise. There is a true old saying, that "love furthers knowledge:" but, above all, it is the living essence of that knowledge which makes poets; the first principle of its existence, increase, activity. Of Burns's fervid affection, his generous, all-embracing Love, we have spoken already, as of the grand distinction of his nature, seen equally in word and deed, in his Life and in his Writings. It were easy to multiply examples. Not man only, but all that environs man in the material and moral universe, is lovely in his sight: "the hoary hawthorn," the "troop of gray plover," the "solitary curlew," are all dear to him—all live in this Earth along with him, and to all he is knit as in mysterious brotherhood. How touching is it, for instance, that, amidst the gloom of personal misery, brooding over the wintry desolation without him and within him, he thinks of the "ourie cattle" and "silly sheep," and their sufferings in the pitiless storm!

"I thought me on the ourie cattle,
Or silly sheep, wha bide this brattle
O' wintry war;
Or thro' the drift, deep-lairing, sprattle,
Beneath a scaur.

Ilk happing bird, wee helpless thing,
That in the merry month o' spring
Delighted me to hear thee sing,
What comes o' thee?
Where wilt thou cow'r thy chittering wing,
And close thy ee?"

The tenant of the mean hut, with its "ragged roof and chinky wall," has a heart to pity even these! This is worth several homilies on Mercy; for it is the voice of Mercy herself. Burns, indeed, lives in sympathy; his soul rushes forth into all realms of being; nothing that has existence can be indifferent to him. The very devil he cannot hate with right orthodoxy!

"But fare you weel, auld Nickie-ben;
O wad ye tak a thought and men'!
Ye aiblins might,—I dinna ken,—
Still hae a stake;
I'm wae to think upo' yon den,
Even for your sake!"

He did not know, probably, that Sterne had been beforehand with him. "'He is the father of curses and lies,' said Dr. Slop; 'and is cursed and damned already.'—'I am sorry for it,' quoth my uncle Toby!"—"A poet without Love, were a physical and metaphysical impossibility."

Why should we speak of *Scots, wha hae wi' Wallace bled*; since all know it, from the king to the meanest of his subjects? This dithyrambic was composed on horseback; in riding in the middle of tempests, over the wildest Galloway moor, in company with a Mr. Syme, who, observing the poet's looks, forebore to speak,—judiciously enough,—for a man composing *Bruce's Address* might be unsafe to trifle with. Doubtless this stern hymn was singing itself, as he formed it, through the soul of Burns; but to the external ear, it should be sung with the throat of the whirlwind. So long as there is warm blood in the heart of a Scotchman or man, it will move in fierce thrills under this war-ode, the best, we believe, that was ever written by any pen.

Another wild, stormful song, that dwells in our ear and mind with a strange tenacity, is *Macpherson's Farewell*. Perhaps there is something in the tradition itself that co-operates. For was not this grim Celt, this shaggy Northland Cacus, that "lived a life of sturt and strife, and died by treacherie," was not he too one of the Nimrods and Napoleons of the earth, in the arena of his own remote misty glens, for want of a clearer and wider one? Nay, was there not a touch of grace given him? A fibre of love and softness, of poetry itself, must have lived in his savage heart; for he composed that air the night before his execution; on the wings of that poor melody, his better soul would soar away above oblivion, pain, and all the ignominy and despair, which, like an avalanche, was hurling him to the abyss! Here, also, as at Thebes, and in Pelops' line, was material Fate matched against man's Free-will; matched in bitterest though obscure duel; and the ethereal soul sunk not, even in its blindness, without a cry which has survived it. But who, except Burns, could have given words to such a soul—words that we never listen to without a strange half-barbarous, half-poetic fellow-feeling?

Sae rantingly, sae wantonly,
Sae dauntingly gaed he;

49

He play'd a spring, and danced it round,
Below the gallows tree.

Under a lighter and thinner disguise, the same principle of
Love, which we have recognized as the great characteristic of
Burns, and of all true poets, occasionally manifests itself in the
shape of Humor. Everywhere, indeed, in his sunny moods, a full
buoyant flood of mirth rolls through the mind of Burns; he rises
to the high, and stoops to the low, and is brother and playmate to
all Nature. We speak not of his bold and often irresistible faculty
of caricature; for this is Drollery rather than Humor: but a much
tenderer sportfulness dwells in him; and comes forth, here and
there, in evanescent and beautiful touches; as in his *Address to the
Mouse*, or the *Farmer's Mare*, or in his *Elegy on Poor Mailie*,
which last may be reckoned his happiest effort of this kind. In
these pieces, there are traits of a Humor as fine as that of Sterne;
yet altogether different, original, peculiar,—the Humor of Burns.
Of the tenderness, the playful pathos, and many other
kindred qualities of Burns's poetry, much more might be said; but
now, with these poor outlines of a sketch, we must prepare to
quit this part of our subject. To speak of his individual writings,
adequately, and with any detail, would lead us far beyond our
limits. As already hinted, we can look on but few of these pieces
as, in strict critical language, deserving the name of Poems; they
are rhymed eloquence, rhymed pathos, rhymed sense; yet seldom
essentially melodious, aerial, poetical. *Tam O'Shanter* itself,
which enjoys so high a favor, does not appear to us, at all
decisively, to come under this last category. It is not so much a
poem, as a piece of sparkling rhetoric; the heart and body of the
story still lies hard and dead. He has not gone back, much less
carried us back, into that dark, earnest wondering age, when the
tradition was believed, and when it took its rise; he does not
attempt, by any new modelling of his supernatural ware, to strike
anew that deep mysterious chord of human nature, which once
responded to such things; and which lives in us too, and will
forever live, though silent, or vibrating with far other notes, and

to far different issues. Our German readers will understand us, when we say, that he is not the Tieck but the Musäus of this tale. Externally it is all green and living; yet look closer, it is no firm growth, but only ivy on a rock. The piece does not properly cohere; the strange chasm which yawns in our incredulous imaginations between the Ayr public-house and the gate of Tophet, is nowhere bridged over, nay, the idea of such a bridge is laughed at; and thus the Tragedy of the adventure becomes a mere drunken phantasmagoria, painted on ale-vapors, and the farce alone has any reality. We do not say that Burns should have made much more of this tradition; we rather think that, for strictly poetical purposes, not much *was* to be made of it. Neither are we blind to the deep, varied, genial power displayed in what he has actually accomplished: but we find far more "Shakspearian" qualities, as these of *Tam O'Shanter* have been fondly named, in many of his other pieces; nay, we incline to believe, that this latter might have been written, all but quite as well, by a man who, in place of genius, had only possessed talent.

Perhaps we may venture to say, that the most strictly poetical of all his "poems" is one, which does not appear in Currie's Edition; but has been often printed before and since, under the humble title of *The Jolly Beggars*. The subject truly is among the lowest in nature; but it only the more shows our poet's gift in raising it into the domain of Art. To our minds, this piece seems thoroughly compacted; melted together, refined; and poured forth in one flood of true *liquid* harmony. It is light, airy, and soft of movement; yet sharp and precise in its details; every face is a portrait: that *raucle carlin*, that *wee Apollo*, that *Son of Mars*, are Scottish, yet ideal; the scene is at once a dream, and the very Rag-castle of "Poosie-Nansie." Farther, it seems in a considerable degree complete, a real self-supporting Whole, which is the highest merit in a poem. The blanket of the night is drawn asunder for a moment; in full, ruddy, and flaming light, these rough tatterdemalions are seen in their boisterous revel; for the strong pulse of Life vindicates its right to gladness even here; and when the curtain closes, we prolong the action without effort; the next day, as the last, our *Caird* and our *Balladmonger* are singing and soldiering; their "brats and callets" are hawking, begging, cheating; and some other night, in new combinations, they will ring from Fate another hour of wassail and good cheer. It would be strange, doubtless, to call this the best of Burns's writings; we mean to say only, that it seems to us the most perfect of its kind, as a piece of poetical composition, strictly so called. In the *Beggar's Opera*, in the *Beggar's Bush*, as other critics have already remarked, there is nothing which, in real poetic vigor, equals this *Cantata*; nothing, as we think, which comes within many degrees of it.

But by far the most finished, complete, and truly inspired pieces of Burns are, without dispute, to be found among his *Songs*. It is here that, although through a small aperture, his light shines with the least obstruction; in its highest beauty, and pure sunny clearness. The reason may be, that Song is a brief and simple species of composition: and requires nothing so much for its perfection as genuine poetic feeling, genuine music of heart. The Song has its rules equally with the Tragedy; rules which in most cases are poorly fulfilled, in many cases are not so much as felt. We might write a long essay on the Songs of Burns; which we reckon by far the best that Britain has yet produced; for, indeed, since the era of Queen Elizabeth, we know not that, by any other hand, aught truly worth attention has been accomplished in this department. True, we have songs enough "by persons of quality;" we have tawdry, hollow, wine-bred, madrigals; many a rhymed "speech" in the flowing and watery vein of Ossorius the Portugal Bishop, rich in sonorous words, and, for moral, dashed perhaps with some tint of a sentimental sensuality; all which many persons cease not from endeavoring to sing: though for most part, we fear, the music is but from the throat outward, or at best from some region far enough short of the *Soul*; not in which, but in a certain inane Limbo of the Fancy, or even in some vaporous debatable land on the outside of the Nervous System, most of such madrigals and rhymed speeches seem to have originated. With the Songs of Burns we must not name these things. Independently of the clear, manly, heartfelt sentiment that ever pervades *his* poetry, his Songs are honest in another point of view: in form as well as in spirit. They do not *affect* to be set to music; but they actually and in themselves are music; they have received their life, and fashioned themselves together, in the medium of Harmony, as Venus rose from the bosom of the sea. The story, the feeling, is not detailed, but suggested; not *said*, or spouted, in rhetorical completeness and coherence; but *sung*, in fitful gushes, in glowing hints, in fantastic breaks, in *warblings* not of the voice only, but of the whole mind. We consider this to be the essence of a song; and that no songs since the little careless catches, and, as it were, drops of song, which Shakspeare has here and there sprinkled over his plays, fulfil this condition in nearly the same degree as most of Burns's do. Such grace and truth of external movement, too, presupposes in general a corresponding force and truth of sentiment, and inward meaning. The Songs of Burns are not more perfect in the former quality than in the latter. With what tenderness he sings, yet with what vehemence and entireness! There is a piercing wail in his sorrow, the purest rapture in his joy: he burns with the sternest ire, or laughs with the loudest or slyest mirth; and yet he is sweet and soft, "sweet as the smile when fond lovers meet, and soft as their parting tear!" If we farther take into account the immense variety of his subjects; how, from the loud flowing revel in *Willie brew'd a peck o' Maut*, to the still, rapt enthusiasm of sadness for *Mary in Heaven*; from the glad kind greeting of *Auld Langsyne*, or the comic archness of *Duncan Gray*, to the fire-eyed fury of *Scots, wha hae wi' Wallace bled*, he has found a tone and words for every mood of man's heart,—it will seem a small praise if we rank him as the first of all our song-writers; for we know not where to find one worthy of being second to him.

It is on his Songs, as we believe, that Burns's chief influence as an author will ultimately be found to depend: nor, if our Fletcher's aphorism is true, shall we account this a small influence. "Let me make the songs of a people," said he, "and you shall make its laws." Surely, if ever any Poet might have equalled himself with Legislators, on this ground, it was Burns. His songs are already part of the mother tongue, not of Scotland only but of Britain, and of the millions that in all the ends of the earth speak a British language. In hut and hall, as the heart unfolds itself in the joy and wo of existence, the name, the voice of that joy and that wo, is the name and voice which Burns has given them. Strictly speaking, perhaps, no British man has so deeply affected the thoughts and feelings of so many men as this solitary and altogether private individual, with means apparently the humblest.

In another point of view, moreover, we incline to think that Burns's influence may have been considerable: we mean, as exerted specially on the Literature of his country, at least on the Literature of Scotland. Among the great changes which British, particularly Scottish literature, has undergone since that period, one of the greatest will be found to consist in its remarkable increase of nationality. Even the English writers, most popular in Burns's time, were little distinguished for their literary patriotism, in this its best sense. A certain attenuated cosmopolitanism had, in good measure, taken place of the old insular home-feeling; literature was, as it were, without any local environment—was not nourished by the affections which spring from a native soil. Our Grays and Glovers seemed to write almost as if *in vacuo*; the thing written bears no mark of place; it is not written so much for Englishmen, as for men; or rather, which is the inevitable result of this, for certain Generalizations which philosophy termed men. Goldsmith is an exception; not so Johnson; the scene of his *Rambler* is little more English than that of his *Rasselas*. But if such was, in some degree, the case with England, it was, in the highest degree, the case with Scotland. In fact, our Scottish literature had, at that period, a very singular aspect; unexampled, so far as we know, except perhaps at Geneva, where the same state of matters appears still to continue. For a long period after Scotland became British, we had no literature: at the date when Addison and Steele were writing their *Spectators*, our good Thomas Boston was writing, with the noblest intent, but alike in defiance of grammar and philosophy, his *Fourfold State of Man*.

Then came the schisms in our National Church, and the fiercer schisms in our Body Politic: Theologic ink, and Jacobite blood, with gaul enough in both cases, seemed to have blotted out the intellect of the country; however, it was only obscured, not obliterated. Lord Kames made nearly the first attempt, and a tolerably clumsy one, at writing English; and, ere long, Hume, Robertson, Smith, and a whole host of followers, attracted hither the eyes of all Europe. And yet in this brilliant resuscitation of our "fervid genius," there was nothing truly Scottish, nothing indigenous; except, perhaps, the natural impetuosity of intellect, which we sometimes claim, and are sometimes upbraided with, as a characteristic of our nation. It is curious to remark that Scotland, so full of writers, had no Scottish culture, nor indeed any English; our culture was almost exclusively French. It was by studying Racine and Voltaire, Batteux and Boileau, that Kames had trained himself to be a critic and philosopher: it was the light of Montesquieu and Mably that guided Robertson in his political speculations: Quesnay's lamp that kindled the lamp of Adam Smith. Hume was too rich a man to borrow; and perhaps he reached on the French more than he was acted on by them: but neither had he aught to do with Scotland; Edinburgh, equally with La Flèche, was but the lodging and laboratory, in which he not so much morally *lived*, as metaphysically *investigated*. Never, perhaps, was there a class of writers, so clear and well-ordered, yet so totally destitute, to all appearance, of any patriotic affection, nay, of any human affection whatever. The French wits of the period were as unpatriotic; but their general deficiency in moral principle, not to say their avowed sensuality and unbelief in all virtue, strictly so called, render this accountable enough. We hope there is a patriotism founded on something better than prejudice; that our country may be dear to us, without injury to our philosophy; that in loving and justly prizing all other lands, we may prize justly, and yet love before all others, our own stern Motherland, and the venerable structure of social and moral Life, which Mind has through long ages been building up for us there. Surely there is nourishment for the better part of man's heart in all this: surely the roots, that have fixed themselves in the very core of man's being, may be so cultivated as to grow up not into briers, but into roses, in the field of his life! Our Scottish sages have no such propensities: the field of their life shows neither briers nor roses; but only a flat, continuous thrashing-floor for Logic, whereon all questions, from the "Doctrine of Rent," to the "Natural History of Religion," are thrashed and sifted with the same mechanical impartiality!

With Sir Walter Scott at the head of our literature, it cannot be denied that much of this evil is past, or rapidly passing away: our chief literary men, whatever other faults they may have, no longer live among us like a French Colony, or some knot of Propaganda Missionaries; but like natural-born subjects of the soil, partaking and sympathizing in all our attachments, humors, and habits. Our literature no longer grows in water, but in mould, and with the true racy virtues of the soil and climate. How much of this change may be due to Burns, or to any other individual, it might be difficult to estimate. Direct literary imitation of Burns was not to be looked for. But his example, in the fearless adoption of domestic subjects, could not but operate from afar; and certainly in no heart did the love of country ever burn with a warmer glow than in that of Burns: "a tide of Scottish prejudice," as he modestly calls this deep and generous feeling, "had been poured along his veins; and he felt that it would boil there till the flood-gates shut in eternal rest." It seemed to him, as if *he* could do so little for his country, and yet would so gladly have done all. One small province stood open for him; that of Scottish song, and how eagerly he entered on it; how devotedly he labored there! In his most toilsome journeyings, this object never quits him; it is the little happy-valley of his careworn heart. In the gloom of his own affliction, he eagerly searches after some lonely brother of the muse, and rejoices to snatch one other name from the oblivion that was covering it! These were early feelings, and they abode with him to the end.

————a wish, (I mind its power,)
A wish, that to my latest hour
Will strongly heave my breast;
That I, for poor auld Scotland's sake,
Some useful plan or book could make,
Or sing a sang at least.
The rough bur Thistle spreading wide
Amang the bearded bear,
I turn'd my weeding-clips aside,
And spared the symbol dear.

But to leave the mere literary character of Burns, which has already detained us too long, we cannot but think that the Life he willed, and was fated to lead among his fellow-men, is both more interesting and instructive than any of his written works. These Poems are but like little rhymed fragments scattered here and there in the grand unrhymed Romance of his earthly existence; and it is only when intercalated in this at their proper places, that they attain their full measure of significance. And this too, alas, was but a fragment! The plan of a mighty edifice had been sketched; some columns, porticoes, firm masses of building, stand completed; the rest more or less clearly indicated; with many a far-stretching tendency, which only studious and friendly eyes can now trace towards the purposed termination. For the work is broken off in the middle, almost in the beginning; and rises among us, beautiful and sad, at once unfinished and a ruin! If charitable judgment was necessary in estimating his poems, and justice required that the aim and the manifest power to fulfil it must often be accepted for the fulfilment; much more is this the case in regard to his life, the sum and result of all his endeavors, where his difficulties came upon him not in detail only, but in mass; and so much has been left unaccomplished, nay, was mistaken, and altogether marred.

Properly speaking, there is but one era in the life of Burns, and that the earliest. We have not youth and manhood; but only youth: for, to the end, we discern no decisive change in the complexion of his character; in his thirty-seventh year, he is still, as it were, in youth. With all that resoluteness of judgment, that penetrating insight, and singular maturity of intellectual power, exhibited in his writings, he never attains to any clearness regarding himself; to the last he never ascertains his peculiar aim, even with such distinctness as is common among ordinary men; and therefore never can pursue it with that singleness of will, which insures success and some contentment to such men. To the last, he wavers between two purposes: glorying in his talent, like a true poet, he yet cannot consent to make this his chief and sole glory, and to follow it as the one thing needful, through poverty or riches, through good or evil report. Another far meaner ambition still cleaves to him; he must dream and struggle about a certain "Rock of Independence;" which, natural and even admirable as it might be, was still but a warring with the world, on the comparitively insignificant ground of his being more or less completely supplied with money, than others; of his standing at a higher, or at a lower altitude in general estimation, than others. For the world still appears to him, as to the young, in borrowed colors; he expects from it what it cannot give to any man; seeks for contentment, not within himself, in action and wise effort, but from without, in the kindness of circumstances, in love, friendship, honor, pecuniary ease. He would be happy, not actively and in himself, but passively, and from some ideal cornucopia of Enjoyments, not earned by his own labor, but showered on him by the beneficence of Destiny. Thus, like a young man, he cannot steady himself for any fixed or systematic pursuit, but swerves to and fro, between passionate hope, and remorseful disappointment: rushing onwards with a deep tempestuous force, he surmounts or breaks asunder many a barrier; travels, nay, advances far, but advancing only under uncertain guidance, is ever and anon turned from his path: and to the last, cannot reach the only true happiness of a man, that of clear, decided Activity in the sphere for which by nature and circumstances he has been fitted and appointed.

We do not say these things in dispraise of Burns: nay, perhaps, they but interest us the more in his favor. This blessing is not given soonest to the best; but rather, it is often the greatest minds that are latest in obtaining it; for where most is to be developed, most time may be required to develope it. A complex condition had been assigned him from without, as complex a condition from within: no "pre-established harmony" existed between the clay soil of Mossgiel and the empyrean soul of Robert Burns; it was not wonderful, therefore, that the adjustment between them should have been long postponed, and his arm long cumbered, and his sight confused, in so vast and discordant an economy, as he had been appointed steward over. Byron was, at his death, but a year younger than Burns; and through life, as it might have appeared, far more simply situated; yet in him, too, we can trace no such adjustment, no such moral manhood; but at best, and only a little before his end, the beginning of what seemed such.

By much the most striking incident in Burns's Life is his journey to Edinburgh; but perhaps a still more important one is his residence at Irvine, so early as in his twenty-third year. Hitherto his life had been poor and toilworn; but otherwise not ungenial, and, with all its distresses, by no means unhappy. In his parentage, deducting outward circumstances, he had every reason to reckon himself fortunate: his father was a man of thoughtful, intense, earnest character, as the best of our peasants are; valuing knowledge, possessing some, and, what is far better and rarer, open-minded for more; a man with a keen insight, and devout heart; reverent towards God, friendly therefore at once, and fearless towards all that God has made; in one word, though but a hard-handed peasant, a complete and fully unfolded *Man*. Such a father is seldom found in any rank in society; and was worth descending far in society to seek. Unfortunately, he was very poor; had he been even a little richer, almost ever so little, the whole might have issued far otherwise. Mighty events turn on a straw; the crossing of a brook decides the conquest of the world. Had this William Burns's small seven acres of nursery ground anywise prospered, the boy Robert had been sent to school; had struggled forward, as so many weaker men do, to some university; come forth not as a rustic wonder, but as a regular well-trained intellectual workman, and changed the whole course of British Literature,—for it lay in him to have done this! But the nursery did not prosper; poverty sank his whole family below the help of even our cheap school-system: Burns remained a hard-worked plough-boy, and British literature took its own course. Nevertheless, even in this rugged scene, there is much to nourish him. If he drudges, it is with his brother, and for his father and mother, whom he loves, and would fain shield from want. Wisdom is not banished from their poor hearth, nor the balm of natural feeling: the solemn words, *Let us Worship God*, are heard there from a "priest-like father;" if threatenings of unjust men throw mother and children into tears, these are tears not of grief only, but of holiest affection; every heart in that humble group feels itself the closer knit to every other; in their hard warfare they are there together, a "little band of brethren." Neither are such tears, and the deep beauty that dwells in them, their only portion. Light visits the hearts as it does the eyes of all living: there is a force, too, in this youth, that enables him to trample on misfortune; nay, to bind it under his feet to make him sport. For a bold, warm, buoyant humor of character has been given him; and so the thick-coming shapes of evil are welcomed with a gay, friendly irony, and in their closest pressure he bates no jot of heart or hope. Vague yearnings of ambition fail not, as he grows up; dreamy fancies hang like cloud-cities around him; the curtain of Existence is slowly rising, in many-colored splendor and gloom: and the auroral light of first love is gilding his horizon, and the music of song is on his path; and so he walks

"——in glory and in joy,
Behind his plough, upon the mountain side!"

We know, from the best evidence, that up to this date, Burns was happy; nay, that he was the gayest, brightest, most fantastic, fascinating being to be found in the world; more so even than he ever afterwards appeared. But now at this early age, he quits the paternal roof; goes forth into looser, louder, more exciting society; and becomes initiated in those dissipations, those vices, which a certain class of philosophers have asserted to be a natural preparative for entering on active life; a kind of mud-bath, in which the youth is, as it were, necessitated to steep, and, we suppose, cleanse himself, before the real toga of Manhood can be laid on him. We shall not dispute much with this class of philosophers; we hope they are mistaken; for Sin and Remorse so easily beset us at all stages of life, and are always such indifferent company, that it seems hard we should, at any stage, be forced and fated not only to meet, but to yield to them; and even serve for a term in their leprous armada. We hope it is not so. Clear we are, at all events, it cannot be the training one receives in this service, but only our determining to desert from it, that fits for true manly Action. We become men, not after we have been dissipated, and disappointed in the chase of false pleasure; but after we have ascertained, in any way, what impassable barriers hem us in through this life; how mad it is to hope for contentment to our infinite soul from the *gifts* of this extremely finite world! that a man must be sufficient for himself; and that "for suffering and enduring there is no remedy but striving and doing." Manhood begins when we have in any way made truce with Necessity; begins, at all events, when we have surrendered to Necessity, as the most part only do; but begins joyfully and hopefully only when we have reconciled ourselves to Necessity; and thus, in reality, triumphed over it, and felt that in Necessity we are free. Surely, such lessons as this last, which, in one shape or other, is the grand lesson for every mortal man, are better learned from the lips of a devout mother, in the looks and actions of a devout father, while the heart is yet soft and pliant, than in collision with the sharp adamant of Fate, attracting us to shipwreck us, when the heart is grown hard, and may be broken before it will become contrite! Had Burns continued to learn this, as he was already learning it, in his father's cottage, he would have learned it fully, which he never did,—and been saved many a lasting aberration, many a bitter hour and year of remorseful sorrow.

It seems to us another circumstance of fatal import in Burns's history, that at this time too he became involved in the religious quarrels of his district; that he was enlisted and feasted, as the fighting man of the New-Light Priesthood, in their highly unprofitable warfare. At the tables of these free-minded clergy, he learned much more than was needful for him. Such liberal ridicule of fanaticism awakened in his mind scruples about Religion itself; and a whole world of Doubts, which it required quite another set of conjurors than these men to exorcise. We do not say that such an intellect as his could have escaped similar doubts, at some period of his history; or even that he could, at a later period, have come through them altogether victorious and unharmed: but it seems peculiarly unfortunate that this time, above all others, should have been fixed for the encounter. For now, with principles assailed by evil example from without, by "passions raging like demons" from within, he had little need of skeptical misgivings to whisper treason in the heat of the battle, or to cut off his retreat if he were already defeated. He loses his feeling of innocence; his mind is at variance with itself; the old divinity no longer presides there; but wild Desires and wild Repentance alternately oppress him. Ere long, too, he has committed himself before the world; his character for sobriety, dear to a Scottish peasant, as few corrupted worldings can even conceive, is destroyed in the eyes of men; and his only refuge consists in trying to disbelieve his guiltiness, and is but a refuge of lies. The blackest desperation now gathers over him, broken only by the red lightnings of remorse. The whole fabric of his life is blasted asunder; for now not only his character, but his personal liberty, is to be lost; men and Fortune are leagued for his hurt; "hungry Ruin has him in the wind." He sees no escape but the saddest of all: exile from his loved country, to a country in every sense inhospitable and abhorrent to him. While the "gloomy night is gathering fast," in mental storm and solitude, as well as in physical, he sings his wild farewell to Scotland:

"Farewell, my friends, farewell my foes!
My peace with these, my love with those:
The bursting tears my heart declare;
Adieu, my native banks of Ayr!"

Light breaks suddenly in on him in floods; but still a false transitory light, and no real sunshine. He is invited to Edinburgh; hastens thither with anticipating heart; is welcomed as in triumph, and with universal blandishment and acclamation; whatever is wisest, whatever is greatest, or loveliest there, gathers round him, to gaze on his face, to show him honor, sympathy, affection. Burns's appearance among the sages and nobles of Edinburgh, must be regarded as one of the most singular phenomena in modern Literature; almost like the appearance of some Napoleon among the crowned sovereigns of modern Politics. For it is nowise as a "mockery king," set there by favor, transiently, and for a purpose, that he will let himself be treated; still less is he a mad Rienzi, whose sudden elevation turns his too weak head; but he stands there on his own basis; cool, unastonished, holding his equal rank from Nature herself; putting forth no claim which there is not strength *in* him, as well as about him, to vindicate. Mr. Lockhart has some forcible observations on this point:

"It needs no effort of imagination," says he, "to conceive what the sensations of an isolated set of scholars (almost all either clergymen or professors) must have been, in the presence of this big-boned, black-browed, brawny stranger, with his great flashing eyes, who, having forced his way among them from the plough-tail, at a single stride, manifested in the whole strain of his bearing and conversation, a most thorough conviction, that in the society of the most eminent men of his nation, he was exactly where he was entitled to be; hardly deigned to flatter them by exhibiting even an occasional symptom of being flattered by their notice; by turns calmly measured himself against the most cultivated understandings of his time in discussion; overpowered the *bon mots* of the most celebrated convivialists by broad floods of merriment, impregnated with all the burning life of genius; astounded bosoms habitually enveloped in the thrice-piled folds of social reserve, by compelling them to tremble,—nay, to tremble visibly,—beneath the fearless touch of natural pathos; and all this without indicating the smallest willingness to be ranked among those professional ministers of excitement, who are content to be paid in money and smiles for doing what the spectators and auditors would be ashamed of doing in their own persons, even if they had the power of doing it; and last, and probably worst of all, who was known to be in the habit of enlivening societies which they would have scorned to approach, still more frequently than their own, with eloquence no less magnificent; with wit, in all likelihood still more daring; often enough as the superiors whom he fronted without alarm might have guessed from the beginning, and had, ere long, no occasion to guess, with wit pointed at themselves."

The farther we remove from this scene, the more singular will it seem to us: details of the exterior aspect of it are already full of interest. Most readers recollect Mr. Walker's personal interviews with Burns as among the best passages of his Narrative; a time will come when this reminiscence of Sir Walter Scott's, slight though it is, will also be precious.

"As for Burns," writes Sir Walter, "I may truly say *Vergilium vidi tantum.* I was a lad of fifteen in 1786-7, when he came first to Edinburgh, but had sense and feeling enough to be much interested in his poetry, and would have given the world to know him: but I had very little acquaintance with any literary people; and still less with the gentry of the west country, the two sets that he most frequented. Mr. Thomas Grierson was at that time a clerk of my father's. He knew Burns, and promised to ask him to his lodgings to dinner, but had no opportunity to keep his word; otherwise I might have seen more of this distinguished man. As it was, I saw him one day at the late venerable Professor Ferguson's, where there were several gentlemen of literary reputation, among whom I remember the celebrated Mr. Dugald Stewart. Of course, we youngsters sat silent, looked and listened. The only thing I remember, which was remarkable in Burns's manner, was the effect produced upon him by a print of Bunbury's, representing a soldier lying dead on the snow, his dog sitting in misery on one side,—on the other, his widow, with a child in her arms. These lines were written beneath:

"Cold on Canadian hills, or Minden's plain,
Perhaps that mother wept her soldier slain:
Bent o'er her babe, her eye dissolved in dew,
The big drops mingling with the milk he drew
Gave the sad presage of his future years,
The child of misery baptized in tears."

"Burns seemed much affected by the print, or rather by the ideas which it suggested to his mind. He actually shed tears. He asked whose the lines were, and it chanced that nobody but myself remembered that they occur in a half-forgotten poem of Langhorne's, called by the unpromising title of "The Justice of Peace." I whispered my information to a friend present, he mentioned it to Burns, who rewarded me with a look and a word, which, though of mere civility, I then received and still recollect with very great pleasure.

"His person was strong and robust; his manners rustic, not clownish; a sort of dignified plainness and simplicity, which received part of its effect perhaps from one's knowledge of his extraordinary talents. His features are represented in Mr. Nasmyth's picture: but to me it conveys the idea that they are diminished, as if seen in perspective. I think his countenance was more massive than it looks in any of the portraits. I should have taken the poet, had I not known what he was, for a very sagacious country farmer of the old Scotch school, *i. e.* none of your modern agriculturists who keep laborers for their drudgery, but the *douce gudeman* who held his own plough. There was a strong expression of sense and shrewdness in all his lineaments; the eye alone, I think, indicated the poetical character and temperament. It was large, and of a dark cast, which glowed (I say literally *glowed*) when he spoke with feeling or interest. I never saw such another eye in a human head, though I have seen the most distinguished men of my time. His conversation expressed perfect self-confidence, without the slightest presumption. Among the men who were the most learned of their time and country, he expressed himself with perfect firmness, but without the least intrusive forwardness; and when he differed in opinion, he did not hesitate to express it firmly, yet at the same time with modesty. I do not remember any part of his conversation distinctly enough to be quoted; nor did I ever see him again, except in the street, where he did not recognize me, as I could not expect he should. He was much caressed in Edinburgh: but (considering what literary emoluments have been since his day) the efforts made for his relief were extremely trifling.

"I remember, on this occasion, I mention, I thought Burns's acquaintance with English poetry was rather limited; and also, that having twenty times the abilities of Allan Ramsay and of Ferguson, he talked of them with too much humility as his models: there was doubtless national predilection in his estimate.

"This is all I can tell you about Burns. I have only to add, that his dress corresponded with his manner. He was like a farmer dressed in his best to dine with the laird. I do not speak in *malam partem*, when I say, I never saw a man in company with his superiors in station or information more perfectly free from either the reality or the affectation of embarrassment. I was told, but did not observe it, that his address to females was extremely deferential, and always with a turn either to the pathetic or humorous, which engaged their attention particularly. I have heard the late Duchess of Gordon remark this. I do not know any thing I can add to these recollections of forty years since."

The conduct of Burns under this dazzling blaze of favor; the calm, unaffected, manly manner, in which he not only bore it, but estimated its value, has justly been regarded as the best proof that could be given of his real vigor and integrity of mind. A little natural vanity, some touches of hypocritical modesty, some glimmerings of affectation, at least some fear of being thought affected, we could have pardoned in almost any man; but no such indication is to be traced here. In his unexampled situation the young peasant is not a moment perplexed; so many strange lights do not confuse him, do not lead him astray. Nevertheless, we cannot but perceive that this winter did him great and lasting injury. A somewhat clearer knowledge of men's affairs, scarcely of their characters, it did afford him: but a sharper feeling of Fortune's unequal arrangements in their social destiny it also left with him. He had seen the gay and gorgeous arena, in which the powerful are born to play their parts; nay, had himself stood in the midst of it; and he felt more bitterly than ever, that here he was but a looker-on, and had no part or lot in that splendid game. From this time a jealous, indignant fear of social degradation takes possession of him; and perverts, so far as aught could pervert, his private contentment, and his feelings towards his richer fellows. It was clear enough to Burns that he had talent enough to make a fortune, or a hundred fortunes, could he but have rightly willed this; it was clear also that he willed something far different, and therefore could not make one. Unhappy it was that he had not power to choose the one, and reject the other; but must halt forever between two opinions, two objects; making hampered advancement towards either. But so is it with many men: we "long for the merchandise, yet would fain keep the price;" and so stand chaffering with Fate in vexatious altercation, till the Night come, and our fair is over!

The Edinburgh learned of that period were in general more noted for clearness of head than for warmth of heart: with the exception of the good old Blacklock, whose help was too ineffectual, scarcely one among them seems to have looked at Burns with any true sympathy, or indeed much otherwise than as at a highly curious *thing*. By the great, also, he is treated in the customary fashion; entertained at their tables, and dismissed: certain modica of pudding and praise are, from time to time, gladly exchanged for the fascination of his presence; which exchange once effected, the bargain is finished, and each party goes his several way. At the end of this strange season, Burns gloomily sums up his gains and losses, and meditates on the chaotic future. In money he is somewhat richer; in fame and the show of happiness, infinitely richer; but in the substance of it, as poor as ever. Nay, poorer, for his heart is now maddened still more with the fever of mere worldly Ambition: and through long years the disease will rack him with unprofitable sufferings, and weaken his strength for all true and nobler aims.

What Burns was next to do or avoid; how a man so circumstanced was now to guide himself towards his true advantage, might at this point of time have been a question for the wisest: and it was a question which he was left altogether to answer for himself: of his learned or rich patrons it had not struck any individual to turn a thought on this so trivial matter. Without claiming for Burns the praise of perfect sagacity, we must say, that his Excise and Farm scheme does not seem to us a very unreasonable one; and that we should be at a loss, even now, to suggest one decidedly better. Some of his admirers, indeed, are scandalized at his ever resolving to *gauge*; and would have had him apparently lie still at the pool, till the spirit of Patronage should stir the waters, and then heal with one plunge all his worldly sorrows! We fear such counsellors knew but little of Burns; and did not consider that happiness might in all cases be cheaply had by waiting for the fulfilment of golden dreams, were it not that in the interim the dreamer must die of hunger. It reflects credit on the manliness and sound sense of Burns, that he felt so early on what ground he was standing; and preferred self-help, on the humblest scale, to dependence and inaction, though with hope of far more splendid possibilities. But even these possibilities were not rejected in his scheme: he might expect, if it chanced that he *had* any friend, to rise, in no long period, into something even like opulence and leisure; while again, if it chanced that he had no friend, he could still live in security; and for the rest, he "did not intend to borrow honor from any profession." We think, then, that his plan was honest and well calculated: all turned on the execution of it. Doubtless it failed; yet not, we believe, from any vice inherent in itself. Nay, after all, it was no failure of external means, but of internal, that overtook Burns. His was no bankruptcy of the purse, but of the soul; to his last day, he owed no man any thing.

Meanwhile he begins well; with two good and wise actions. His donation to his mother, munificent from a man whose income had lately been seven pounds a year, was worthy of him, and not more than worthy. Generous also, and worthy of him, was his treatment of the woman whose life's welfare now depended on his pleasure. A friendly observer might have hoped serene days for him: his mind is on the true road to peace with itself: what clearness he still wants will be given as he proceeds; for the best teacher of duties, that still lie dim to us, is the Practice of those we see, and have at hand. Had the "patrons of genius," who could give him nothing, but taken nothing from him, at least nothing more!—the wounds of his heart would have healed, vulgar ambition would have died away. Toil and Frugality would have been welcome, since Virtue dwelt with them, and poetry would have shone through them as of old; and in her clear ethereal light, which was his own by birth-right, he might have looked down on his earthly destiny, and all its obstructions, not with patience only, but with love.

But the patrons of genius would not have it so. Picturesque tourists,[2] all manner of fashionable danglers after literature, and,

---

[2] There is one little sketch certain "English gentlemen" of this class, which, though adopted in Currie's Narrative, and since then repeated in most others, we have all along felt an invincible disposition to regard as imaginary: "On a rock that projected into the stream they saw a man employed in angling, of a singular appearance. He had a cap made of fox-skin on his head, a loose great-coat fixed round him by a belt, from which depended an enormous Highland broad-sword. It was Burns." Now, we rather think, it was not Burns. For, to say nothing of the fox-skin cap, loose and quite Hibernian watch-coat with the belt, what are we to make of this "enormous Highland broad-sword" depending from him? More especially, as there is no word of parish constables on the outlook to see whether, as Dennis phrases it, he had an eye to his own midriff, or that of the public! Burns, of all men, had the least tendency to seek

far worse, all manner of convivial Mecænases, hovered round him in his retreat; and his good as well as his weak qualities secured them influence over him. He was flattered by their notice; and his warm social nature made it impossible for him to shake them off, and hold on his way apart from them. These men, as we believe, were proximately the means of his ruin. Not that they meant him any ill; they only meant themselves a little good; if he suffered harm, let *him* look to it! But they wasted his precious time and his precious talent; they disturbed his composure, broke down his returning habits of temperance and assiduous contented exertion. Their pampering was baneful to him; their cruelty, which soon followed, was equally baneful. The old grudge against Fortune's inequality awoke with new bitterness in their neighborhood, and Burns had no retreat but to the "Rock of Independence," which is but an air-castle, after all, that looks well at a distance, but will screen no one from real wind and wet. Flushed with irregular excitement, exasperated alternately by contempt of others, and contempt of himself, Burns was no longer regaining his peace of mind, but fast losing it forever. There was a hollowness at the heart of his life, for his conscience did not now approve what he was doing.

Amid the vapors of unwise enjoyment, of bootless remorse, and angry discontent with Fate, his true loadstar, a life of Poetry, with Poverty, nay, with Famine if it must be so, was too often altogether hidden from his eyes. And yet he sailed a sea, where, without some such guide, there was no right steering. Meteors of French Politics rise before him, but these were not *his* stars. An accident this, which hastened, but did not originate, his worst distresses. In the mad contentions of that time, he comes in collision with certain official Superiors; is wounded by them; cruelly lacerated, we should say, could a dead mechanical implement, in any case, be called cruel: and shrinks, in indignant pain, into deeper self-seclusion, into gloomier moodiness than

for distinction, either in his own eyes, or those of others, by such poor mummeries.

ever. His life has now lost its unity: it is a life of fragments; led with little aim, beyond the melancholy one of securing its own continuance—in fits of wild false joy, when such offered, and of black despondency when they passed away. His character before the world begins to suffer: calumny is busy with him; for a miserable man makes more enemies than friends. Some faults he has fallen into, and a thousand misfortunes; but deep criminality is what he stands accused of, and they that are *not* without sin, cast the first stone at him! For is he not a well-wisher of the French Revolution, a Jacobin, and therefore in that one act guilty of all? These accusations, political and moral, it has since appeared, were false enough; but the world hesitated little to credit them. Nay, his convivial Mecænases themselves were not the last to do it. There is reason to believe that, in his later years, the Dumfries Aristocracy had partly withdrawn themselves from Burns, as from a tainted person, no longer worthy of their acquaintance. That painful class, stationed, in all provincial cities, behind the outmost breastwork of Gentility, there to stand siege and do battle against the intrusion of Grocerdom, and Grazierdom, had actually seen dishonor in the society of Burns, and branded him with their veto; had, as we vulgarly say, *cut* him! We find one passage in this work of Mr. Lockhart's, which will not out of our thoughts:

"A gentleman of that country, whose name I have already more than once had occasion to refer to, has often told me that he was seldom more grieved, than when, riding into Dumfries one fine summer evening about this time to attend a country ball, he saw Burns walking alone, on the shady side of the principal street of the town, while the opposite side was gay with successive groups of gentlemen and ladies, all drawn together for the festivities of the night, not one of whom appeared willing to recognize him. The horseman dismounted, and joined Burns, who, on his proposing to cross the street, said: 'Nay, nay, my young friend, that's all over now;' and quoted, after a pause, some verses of Lady Grizzel Baillie's pathetic ballad:

'His bonnet stood ance fu' fair on his brow,
His auld ane looked better than mony ane's new;
But now he lets 't wear ony way it will hing,
And casts himsell dowie upon the corn-bing.

'O were we young, as we ance hae been,
We sud hae been galloping down on yon green,
  And linking it ower the lily-white lea!
And werena my heart light I wad die.'

    It was little in Burns's character to let his feelings on certain subjects escape in this fashion. He, immediately after reciting these verses, assumed the sprightliness of his most pleasing manner; and, taking his young friend home with him, entertained him very agreeably till the hour of the ball arrived."

    Alas! when we think that Burns now sleeps "where bitter indignation can no longer lacerate his heart,"[3] and that most of these fair dames and frizzled gentlemen already lie at his side, where the breastwork of gentility is quite thrown down,—who would not sigh over the thin delusions and foolish toys that divide heart from heart, and make man unmerciful to his brother!

    It was not now to be hoped that the genius of Burns would ever reach maturity, or accomplish ought worthy of itself. His spirit was jarred in its melody; not the soft breath of natural feeling, but the rude hand of Fate, was now sweeping over the strings. And yet what harmony was in him, what music even in his discords! How the wild tones had a charm for the simplest and the wisest; and all men felt and knew that here also was one of the Gifted! "If he entered an inn at midnight, after all the inmates were in bed, the news of his arrival circulated from the cellar to the garret; and ere ten minutes had elapsed, the landlord and all his guests were assembled!" Some brief, pure moments of poetic life were yet appointed him, in the composition of his Songs. We can understand how he grasped at this employment; and how, too, he spurned at all other reward for it but what the labor itself

---

[3] *Ubi sæva indignatio cor ulterius lacerare nequit.*—Swift's Epitaph.

brought him. For the soul of Burns, though scathed and marred, was yet living in its full moral strength, though sharply conscious of its errors and abasement: and here, in his destitution and degradation, was one act of seeming nobleness and self-devotedness left even for him to perform. He felt, too, that with all the "thoughtless follies" that had "laid him low," the world was unjust and cruel to him; and he silently appealed to another and calmer time. Not as a hired soldier, but as a patriot, would he strive for the glory of his country; so he cast from him the poor sixpence a-day, and served zealously as a volunteer. Let us not grudge him this last luxury of his existence; let him not have appealed to us in vain! The money was not necessary to him; he struggled through without it; long since, these guineas would have been gone, and now the high-mindedness of refusing them will plead for him in all hearts for ever.

We are here arrived at the crisis of Burns's life; for matters had now taken such a shape with him as could not long continue. If improvement was not to be looked for, Nature could only for a limited time maintain this dark and maddening warfare against the world and itself. We are not medically informed whether any continuance of years was, at this period, probable for Burns; whether his death is to be looked on as in some sense an accidental event, or only as the natural consequence of the long series of events that had preceded. The latter seems to be the likelier opinion; and yet it is by no means a certain one. At all events, as we have said, *some* change could not be very distant. Three gates of deliverance, it seems to us, were open for Burns: clear poetical activity, madness, or death. The first, with longer life, was still possible, though not probable; for physical causes were beginning to be concerned in it: and yet Burns had an iron resolution; could he but have seen and felt, that not only his highest glory, but his first duty, and the true medicine for all his woes, lay here. The second was still less probable; for his mind was ever among the clearest and firmest. So the milder third gate was opened for him: and he passed, not softly, yet speedily, into that still country, where the hail-storms and fire-showers do not reach, and the heaviest-laden wayfarer at length lays down his load!

Contemplating this sad end of Burns, and how he sank unaided by any real help, uncheered by any wise sympathy, generous minds have sometimes figured to themselves, with a reproachful sorrow, that much might have been done for him; that by counsel, true affection, and friendly ministrations, he might have been saved to himself and the world. We question whether there is not more tenderness of heart than soundness of judgment in these suggestions. It seems dubious to us whether the richest, wisest, most benevolent individual, could have lent Burns any effectual help. Counsel, which seldom profits any one, he did not need; in his understanding, he knew the right from the wrong, as well perhaps as any man ever did; but the persuasion, which would have availed him, lies not so much in the head, as in the heart, where no argument or expostulation could have assisted much to implant it. As to money again, we do not really believe that this was his essential want; or well see how any private man could, even presupposing Burns's consent, have bestowed on him an independent fortune, with much prospect of decisive advantage. It is a mortifying truth, that two men in any rank of society could hardly be found virtuous enough to give money, and to take it, as a necessary gift, without injury to the moral entireness of one or both. But so stands the fact: friendship, in the old heroic sense of that term, no longer exists; except in the cases of kindred or other legal affinity; it is in reality no longer expected, or recognized as a virtue among men. A close observer of manners has pronounced "Patronage," that is, pecuniary or other economic furtherance, to be "twice cursed;" cursing him that gives, and him that takes! And thus, in regard to outward matters also, it has become the rule, as in regard to inward it always was and must be the rule, that no one shall look for effectual help to another; but that each shall rest contented with what help he can afford himself. Such, we say, is the principle of modern Honor; naturally enough growing out of that sentiment of Pride, which we inculcate and encourage as the basis of our whole social morality. Many a poet has been poorer than Burns; but no one was ever prouder: and we may question, whether, without great precautions, even a pension from Royalty would not have galled and encumbered, more than actually assisted him.

Still less, therefore, are we disposed to join with another class of Burns's admirers, who accuse the higher ranks among us of having ruined Burns by their selfish neglect of him. We have already stated our doubts whether direct pecuniary help, had it been offered, would have been accepted, or could have proved very effectual. We shall readily admit, however, that much was to be done for Burns; that many a poisoned arrow might have been warded from his bosom; many an entanglement in his path cut asunder by the hand of the powerful; and light and heat shed on him from high places, would have made his humble atmosphere more genial; and the softest heart then breathing might have lived and died with some fewer pangs. Nay, we shall grant further, and for Burns it is granting much, that with all his pride, he would have thanked, even with exaggerated gratitude, any one who had cordially befriended him: patronage, unless once cursed, needed not to have been twice so. At all events, the poor promotion he desired in his calling might have been granted: it was his own scheme, therefore likelier than any other to be of service. All this it might have been a luxury, nay, it was a duty, for our nobility to have done. No part of all this, however, did any of them do; or apparently attempt, or wish to do; so much is granted against them. But what then is the amount of their blame? Simply that they were men of the world, and walked by the principles of such men; that they treated Burns, as other nobles and other commoners had done other poets; as the English did Shakspeare; as King Charles and his cavaliers did Butler, as King Philip and his Grandees did Cervantes. Do men gather grapes of thorns? or shall we cut down our thorns for yielding only a *fence*, and haws? How, indeed, could the "nobility and gentry of his native land" hold out any help to this "Scottish Bard, proud of his name and country?" Were the nobility and gentry so much as able rightly to help themselves? Had they not their game to preserve; their borough interests to strengthen; dinners, therefore, of various kinds to eat and give? Were their means more than adequate to all this business, or less than adequate? Less than adequate in general: few of them in reality were richer than Burns; many of them were poorer; for sometimes they had to wring their supplies, as with thumbscrews, from the hard hand; and, in their need of guineas, to forget their duty of mercy; which Burns was never reduced to do. Let us pity and forgive them. The game they preserved and shot, the dinners they ate and gave, the borough interests they strengthened, the *little* Babylons they severally builded by the glory of their might, are all melted, or melting back into the primeval Chaos, as man's merely selfish endeavors are fated to do: and here was an action extending, in virtue of its worldly influence, we may say, through all time; in virtue of its moral nature, beyond all time, being immortal as the Spirit of Goodness itself; this action was offered them to do, and light was not given them to do it. Let us pity and forgive them. But, better than pity, let us go and *do otherwise.* Human suffering did not end with the life of Burns; neither was the solemn mandate, "Love one another, bear one another's burdens," given to the rich only, but to all men. True, we shall find no Burns to relieve, to assuage by our aid or our pity: but celestial natures, groaning under the fardels of a weary life, we shall still find; and that wretchedness which Fate has rendered *voiceless* and *tuneless,* is not the least wretched, but the most.

Still we do not think that the blame of Burns's failure lies chiefly with the world. The world, it seems to us, treated him with more, rather than with less kindness, than it usually shows to such men. It has ever, we fear, shown but small favor to its Teachers; hunger and nakedness, perils and reviling, the prison, the cross, the poison-chalice, have, in most times and countries, been the market-place it has offered for Wisdom, the welcome with which it has greeted those who have come to enlighten and purify it. Homer and Socrates, and the Christian Apostles belong to old days; but the world's Martyrology was not completed with these. Roger Bacon and Galileo languish in priestly dungeons,

Tasso pines in the cell of a madhouse, Camoens dies begging on the streets of Lisbon. So neglected, so "persecuted they the Prophets," not in Judea only, but in all places where men have been. We reckon that every poet of Burns's order is, or should be, a prophet and teacher to his age; that he has no right therefore to expect great kindness from it, but rather is bound to do it great kindness; that Burns, in particular, experienced fully the usual proportion of the world's goodness; and that the blame of his failure, as we have said, lies not chiefly with the world.

Where then does it lie? We are forced to answer: With himself; it is his inward, not his outward misfortunes, that bring him to the dust. Seldom, indeed, is it otherwise; seldom is a life morally wrecked, but the grand cause lies in some internal mal-arrangement, some want less of good fortune than of good guidance. Nature fashions no creature without implanting in it the strength needful for its action and duration; least of all does she so neglect her masterpiece and darling, the poetic soul. Neither can we believe that it is in the power of *any* external circumstances utterly to ruin the mind of a man; nay, if proper wisdom be given him, even so much as to affect its essential health and beauty. The sternest sum-total of all worldly misfortunes is Death; nothing more *can* lie in the cup of human wo: yet many men, in all ages, have triumphed over Death, and led it captive; converting its physical victory into a moral victory for themselves, into a seal and immortal consecration for all that their past life had achieved. What has been done, may be done again; nay, it is but the degree and not the kind of such heroism that differs in different seasons; for without some portion of this spirit, not of boisterous daring, but of silent fearlessness, of Self-denial, in all its forms, no good man, in any scene or time, has ever attained to be good.

We have already stated the error of Burns; and mourned over it, rather than blamed it. It was the want of unity in his purposes, of consistency in his aims; the hapless attempt to mingle in friendly union the common spirit of the world with the spirit of poetry, which is of a far different and altogether irreconcilable nature. Burns was nothing wholly, and Burns could be nothing; no man formed as he was can be any thing, by halves. The heart, not of a mere hot-blooded, popular verse-monger, or poetical *Restaurateur*, but of a true Poet and Singer, worthy of the old religious heroic times, had been given him: and he fell in an age, not of heroism and religion, but of skepticism, selfishness, and triviality, when true Nobleness was little understood, and its place supplied by a hollow, dissocial, altogether barren and unfruitful principle of Pride. The influences of that age, his open, kind, susceptible nature, to say nothing of his highly untoward situation, made it more than usually difficult for him to repel or resist; the better spirit that was within him ever sternly demanded its rights, its supremacy; he spent his life in endeavoring to reconcile these two; and lost it, as he must have lost it, without reconciling them here.

Burns was born poor; and born also to continue poor, for he would not endeavor to be otherwise: this it had been well could he have once for all admitted, and considered as finally settled. He was poor, truly; but hundreds even of his own class and order of minds have been poorer, yet have suffered nothing deadly from it: nay, his own father had a far sorer battle with ungrateful destiny than his was; and he did not yield to it, but died courageously warring, and to all moral intents prevailing, against it. True, Burns had little means, had even little time for poetry, his only real pursuit and vocation; but so much the more precious was what little he had. In all these external respects his case was hard; but very far from the hardest. Poverty, incessant drudgery, and much worse evils, it has often been the lot of poets and wise men to strive with, and their glory to conquer. Locke was banished as a traitor; and wrote his *Essay on the Human Understanding*, sheltering himself in a Dutch garret. Was Milton rich or at his ease, when he composed *Paradise Lost*? Not only low, but fallen from a height; not only poor, but impoverished; in darkness and with dangers compassed round, he sang his immortal song, and found fit audience, though few. Did not Cervantes finish his work, a maimed soldier, and in prison? Nay, was not the *Araucana*, which Spain acknowledges as its Epic, written without even the aid of paper; scraps of leather, as the stout fighter and voyager snatched any moment from that wild warfare?

And what then had these men, which Burns wanted? Two things; both which, it seems to us, are indispensable for such men. They had a true, religious principle of morals; and a single not a double aim in their activity. They were not self-seekers and self-worshippers; but seekers and worshippers of something far better than Self. Not personal enjoyment was their object; but a high, heroic idea of Religion, of Patriotism, of heavenly Wisdom, in one or the other form, ever hovered before them; in which cause, they neither shrunk from suffering, nor called on the earth to witness it as something wonderful; but patiently endured, counting it blessedness enough so to spend and be spent. Thus the "golden calf of Self-love," however curiously carved, was not their Deity; but the Invisible Goodness, which alone is man's reasonable service. This feeling was as a celestial fountain, whose streams refreshed into gladness and beauty all the provinces of their otherwise too desolate existence. In a word, they willed one thing, to which all other things were subordinated, and made subservient; and therefore they accomplished it. The wedge will rend rocks; but its edge must be sharp and single: if it be double, the wedge is bruised in pieces and will rend nothing.

Part of this superiority these men owed to their age; in which heroism and devotedness were still practised, or at least not yet disbelieved in; but much of it likewise they owed to themselves. With Burns again it was different. His morality, in most of its practical points, is that of a mere worldly man; enjoyment, in a finer or a coarser shape, is the only thing he longs and strives for. A noble instinct sometimes raises him above this; but an instinct only, and acting only for moments. He has no Religion; in the shallow age, where his days were cast, Religion was not discriminated from the New and Old Light *forms* of Religion; and was, with these, becoming obsolete in the minds of men. His heart, indeed, is alive with a trembling adoration, but there is no temple in his understanding. He lives in darkness and in the shadow of doubt. His religion, at best, is an anxious wish; like that of Rabelais, "a great Perhaps."

He loved Poetry warmly, and in his heart; could he but have loved it purely, and with his whole undivided heart, it had been well. For Poetry, as Burns could have followed it, is but another form of Wisdom, of Religion; is itself Wisdom and Religion. But this also was denied him. His poetry is a stray vagrant gleam, which will not be extinguished within him, yet rises not to be the true light of his path, but is often a wildfire that misleads him. It was not necessary for Burns to be rich, to be, or to seem, "independent;" but *it was* necessary for him to be at one with his own heart; to place what was highest in his nature, highest also in his life; "to seek within himself for that consistency and sequence, which external events would for ever refuse him." He was born a poet; poetry was the celestial element of his being, and should have been the soul of his whole endeavors. Lifted into that serene ether, whither he had wings given him to mount, he would have needed no other elevation: Poverty, neglect, and all evil, save the desecration of himself and his Art, were a small matter to him; the pride and the passions of the world lay far beneath his feet; and he looked down alike on noble and slave, on prince and beggar, and all that wore the stamp of man, with clear recognition, with brotherly affection, with sympathy, with pity. Nay, we question whether for his culture as a Poet, poverty, and much suffering for a season, were not absolutely advantageous. Great men, in looking back over their lives, have testified to that effect. "I would not for much," says Jean Paul, "that I had been born richer." And yet Paul's birth was poor enough; for, in another place, he adds; "The prisoner's allowance is bread and water; and I had often only the latter." But the gold that is refined in the hottest furnace comes out the purest; or, as he has himself expressed it, "the canary-bird sings sweeter the longer it has been trained in a darkened cage."

A man like Burns might have divided his hours between poetry and virtuous industry; industry which all true feeling sanctions, nay prescribes, and which has a beauty, for that cause, beyond the pomp of thrones: but to divide his hours between poetry and rich men's banquets, was an ill-starred and inauspicious attempt. How could he be at ease at such banquets? What had he to do there, mingling his music with the coarse roar of altogether earthly voices, and brightening the thick smoke of intoxication with fire lent him from heaven? Was it his aim to *enjoy* life? To-morrow he must go drudge as an Exciseman! We wonder not that Burns became moody, indignant, and at times an offender against certain rules of society; but rather that he did not grow utterly frantic, and run *a-muck* against them all. How could a man, so falsely placed, by his own or others' fault, ever know contentment or peaceable diligence for an hour? What he did, under such perverse guidance, and what he forbore to do, alike fill us with astonishment at the natural strength and worth of his character.

Doubtless there was a remedy for this perverseness: but not in others; only in himself; least of all in simple increase of wealth and worldly "respectability." We hope we have now heard enough about the efficacy of wealth for poetry, and to make poets happy. Nay, have we not seen another instance of it in these very days? Byron, a man of endowment considerably less ethereal than that of Burns, is born in the rank not of a Scottish ploughman, but of an English peer: the highest worldly honors, the fairest worldly career, are his by inheritance: the richest harvest of fame he soon reaps, in another province, by his own hand. And what does all this avail him? Is he happy, is he good, is he true? Alas, he has a poet's soul, and strives towards the Infinite and the Eternal; and soon feels that all this is but mounting to the house-top to reach the stars! Like Burns, he is only a proud man; might like him have "purchased a pocket-copy of Milton to study the character of Satan;" for Satan also is Byron's grand exemplar, the hero of his poetry, and the model apparently of his conduct. As in Burns's case, too, the celestial element will not mingle with the clay of earth; both poet and man of the world he must not be; vulgar Ambition will not live kindly with poetic Adoration; he *cannot* serve God and Mammon. Byron, like Burns, is not happy;

nay, he is the most wretched of all men. His life is falsely arranged: the fire that is in him is not a strong, still, central fire, warming into beauty the products of a world; but it is the mad fire of a volcano; and now,—we look sadly into the ashes of a crater, which ere long, will fill itself with snow!

Byron and Burns were sent forth as missionaries to their generation, to teach it a higher doctrine, a purer truth: they had a message to deliver, which left them no rest till it was accomplished; in dim throes of pain, this divine behest lay smouldering within them; for they knew not what it meant, and felt it only in mysterious anticipation, and they had to die without articulately uttering it. They are in the camp of the Unconverted. Yet not as high messengers of rigorous though benignant truth, but as soft flattering singers, and in pleasant fellowship, will they live there; they are first adulated, then persecuted; they accomplish little for others; they find no peace for themselves, but only death and the peace of the grave. We confess, it is not without a certain mournful awe that we view the fate of these noble souls, so richly gifted, yet ruined to so little purpose with all their gifts. It seems to us there is a stern moral taught in this piece of history,—*twice* told us in our own time! Surely to men of like genius, if there be any such, it carries with it a lesson of deep impressive significance. Surely it would become such a man, furnished for the highest of all enterprises, that of being the Poet of his Age, to consider well what it is that he attempts, and in what spirit he attempts it. For the words of Milton are true in all times, and were never truer than in this: "He, who would write heroic poems, must make his whole life a heroic poem." If he cannot first so make his life, then let him hasten from this arena; for neither its lofty glories, nor its fearful perils, are for him. Let him dwindle into a modish balladmonger; let him worship and be-sing the idols of the time, and the time will not fail to reward him,—if, indeed, he can endure to live in that capacity! Byron and Burns could not live as idol-priests, but the fire of their own hearts consumed them; and better it was for them that they could not. For it is not in the favor of the great, or of the small, but in a life of truth, and in the inexpugnable citadel of his own soul, that a Byron's or a Burns's strength must lie. Let the great stand aloof from him, or know how to reverence him. Beautiful is the union of wealth with favor and furtherance for literature; like the costliest flower-jar enclosing the loveliest amaranth. Yet let not the relation be mistaken. A true poet is not one whom they can hire by money or flattery to be a minister of their pleasures, their writer of occasional verses, their purveyor of table-wit; he cannot be their menial, he cannot even be their partisan. At the peril of both parties, let no such union be attempted! Will a Courser of the Sun work softly in the harness of a Drayhorse? His hoofs are of fire, and his path is through the heavens, bringing light to all lands; will he lumber on mud highways, dragging ale for earthly appetites, from door to door?

But we must stop short in these considerations, which would lead us to boundless lengths. We had something to say on the public moral character of Burns; but this also we must forbear. We are far from regarding him as guilty before the world, as guiltier than the average; nay, from doubting that he is less guilty than one of ten thousand. Tried at a tribunal far more rigid than that where the *Plebiscita* of common civic reputations are pronounced, he has seemed to us even there less worthy of blame than of pity and wonder. But the world is habitually unjust in its judgments of such men; unjust on many grounds, of which this one may be stated as the substance: it decides, like a court of law, by dead statutes; and not positively but negatively; less on what is done right, than on what is, or is not, done wrong. Not the few inches of reflection from the mathematical orbit, which are so easily measured, but the *ratio* of these to the whole diameter, constitutes the real aberration. This orbit may be a planet's, its diameter the breadth of the solar system; or it may be a city hippodrome; nay, the circle of a ginhorse, its diameter a score of feet or paces. But the inches of deflection only are measured; and it is assumed that the diameter of the ginhorse, and that of the planet, will yield the same ratio when compared with them. Here lies the root of many a blind, cruel condemnation of Burnses,

Swifts, Rousseaus, which one never listens to with approval. Granted, the ship comes into harbor with shrouds and tackle damaged; and the pilot is therefore blameworthy; for he has not been all-wise and all-powerful; but to know *how* blameworthy, tell us first whether his voyage has been round the Globe, or only to Ramsgate and the Isle of Dogs.

With our readers in general, with men of right feeling anywhere, we are not required to plead for Burns. In pitying admiration, he lies enshrined in all our hearts, in a far nobler mausoleum than that one of marble; neither will his Works, even as they are, pass away from the memory of man. While the Shakspeares and Miltons roll on like mighty rivers through the country of Thought, bearing fleets of traffickers and assiduous pearl-fishers on their waves; this little Valclusa Fountain will also arrest our eye: for this also is of Nature's own and most cunning workmanship, bursts from the depths of the earth, with a full gushing current, into the light of day; and often will the traveller turn aside to drink of its clear waters, and muse among its rocks and pines!

THE END.